Images of

LONDON
HIDDEN INTERIORS

ENGLISH HERITAGE

Images of
LONDON
HIDDEN INTERIORS

Philip Davies

Photography by
Derek Kendall

ATLANTIC PUBLISHING

To all those in the London Region of English Heritage, and its predecessor, the GLC Historic Buildings Division, without whose dedication and skill many of the buildings illustrated here would no longer exist. London owes them a great debt.

Published by Atlantic Publishing in 2014

Atlantic Publishing
38 Copthorne Road, Croxley Green
Hertfordshire, WD3 4AQ, UK

© Atlantic Publishing 2014
Text © Philip Davies
Photographs © English Heritage — see page 144

A catalogue record is available for this book from the British Library

ISBN 978-1-909242-43-2

Printed and bound in the United Kingdom

Author's note

Most of the places listed in this book are not open to the general public though may have special open days or participate in Open House, London. Each entry includes the street address, postcode and its listed status at the time of going to press, Grade I, Grade II* or Grade II. SAM indicates a Scheduled Ancient Monument. (For further explanation of the National Heritage List for England, visit the English Heritage website.)

The related website www.londonhiddeninteriors. co.uk indicates any public access and gives links to information, where available, for each entry in the book. We remind readers that where the places listed in this book are occupied by individuals or companies, their privacy should be respected at all times.

CONTENTS

INTRODUCTION

Almost exactly a year after the outbreak of the Second World War, on Black Saturday, 7 September 1940, an armada of 1,000 German planes appeared over the city in a formation so vast it spread over 800 square miles and blocked out the sun. When they departed, large areas of the docks and the East End lay ablaze, and over 2,000 Londoners lay dead or seriously injured in the smouldering ruins below.

The level of devastation was immense – on a scale not seen since the Great Fire of London in 1666. Acres of London were laid waste. One in six of its buildings was damaged or destroyed, and many of its most treasured historic buildings and landmarks lay in ruins. In the City of London over one-third of the structures were levelled. Twenty of the City's 47 churches were gutted, along with 17 historic livery company halls. Six more were badly damaged, although miraculously the Apothecaries, Ironmongers and Vintners escaped. The ancient halls and libraries of Inner Temple and Gray's Inn were destroyed, and Middle Temple Hall and Staple Inn bombed. London's historic docks were devastated, and the Guildhall, the Palace of Westminster, Lambeth Palace and the British Museum all severely damaged. Given the remorseless pace of change from 1870 onwards, and the catastrophic damage inflicted during the Second World War, one might be forgiven for thinking that much of London's architectural heritage had been obliterated, and that what survived was given the *coup de grace* by insensitive post-war planning and architecture. But this is not the case.

Many historic buildings, of course, survived intact, if somewhat battered and frayed, and after the war many of those which had been ravaged by bombing were restored – quietly, painstakingly and with great sensitivity; not least the Palace of Westminster, Buckingham Palace, the Guildhall and a dozen or so Wren churches. But it was not just the famous set pieces that benefited; elsewhere, at a time of great national shortages, bold decisions were taken to reinstate many other historic buildings and their priceless interiors with skill and craftsmanship as a very visible symbol of national resurgence. As a consequence a wealth of treasures can still be found hidden behind London's inscrutable façades about which the public knows little, or of which it is only dimly aware.

In contrast to the perceived lack of concern at the loss of so much of London's heritage in the first part of the 20th century, today there is unprecedented public interest in its history and buildings and, not least, what lies behind closed doors inside the offices, institutions, clubs and private houses that so many pass unwittingly every day; from the discreet grandeur of Whitehall and clubland to the fascinating subterranean spaces that lie beneath the capital. The hugely popular annual Open House London event has created access to over 750 buildings and places normally closed to the public and now attracts over a quarter of a million visitors.

This book features more than 60 properties from *London: Hidden Interiors'* 180 examples, to give a range of building types that convey the richness and diversity of London's architectural heritage, and the secrets that lie within. Many of the buildings are private and not open to the public. Where limited or full public access is possible, details can be found on the website at www. londonhiddeninteriors.co.uk.

The selection is an entirely personal one. It concentrates generally on the buildings and interiors that are lesser known and to which the public are not normally allowed – the hidden and the unusual, the quirky and the eccentric – although there is space too for some of the better known. A number celebrate unsung conservation successes of recent years, which deserve greater recognition.

Below: The Central Criminal Court, commonly known as the Old Bailey, with its distinctive dome modelled on the Royal Naval College at Greenwich, was severely damaged by a bomb in May 1941.

Many of London's finest interiors are well known, or readily accessible to the public or the inquisitive observer, and for that reason much of the familiar has been excluded. Interiors are particularly vulnerable to the whims of their owners and the vicissitudes of fashion. Some of the buildings illustrated owe their existence to enlightened patronage, private endeavour, public lobbying, individual enthusiasm or sheer accident, but the principal reason why so many survive is statutory protection.

Architectural conservation is one of the great cultural success stories of the past century. What started off as a *cri de coeur* from amateur enthusiasts and social reformers at the end of the 19th century grew steadily in to a mass movement linked to progressive ideas of town planning and social change. Effective action took a long time to achieve in the face of fierce opposition from vested interests, but it was the scale of wartime losses that helped to prompt decisive action.

In 1947 a national system for the listing of buildings was introduced. Twenty years later the concept of extending similar considerations to whole places through the designation of conservation areas was pioneered by Duncan Sandys. As the chair of a wartime cabinet committee on V1 flying bombs and V2 rockets, Sandys had seen first hand the extent of damage to the national heritage. As a passionate enthusiast, he vowed to protect what remained from comprehensive redevelopment in favour of a much more discriminating approach, starting with an understanding of the value of what already exists. In 1968 this sea change in government attitudes paved the way for the introduction of a coherent system of statutory protection, and the need for prior listed building consent for any works which affect the character or appearance of listed buildings, irrespective of their grade, externally or internally. By recognising them as complete entities, for over 40 years this highly flexible process has saved countless buildings and their interiors from demolition or uninformed alterations. The system has ensured that those areas which contribute to the total significance of a building are protected properly, while facilitating well-informed change to those parts of lesser importance. As a result Britain leads the world in the management of its historic environment.

This book is a plea for an appreciation of all traditions and styles, and a moving on from the style wars which have perpetually bedevilled rational discussion about architecture and new design in historic places. One of the great fallacies of the 20th century was the myth that architecture should be "of its time" and somehow express the "spirit of the age", or Zeitgeist, ignoring the very obvious fact that anything built in any age ipso facto must be representative in some way of its time. The corollary of this has been the very damaging belief that it is somehow "dishonest" to design new buildings that draw their inspiration and vocabulary from the

Above: The Criterion Restaurant, Piccadilly. In 1983 the Formica-covered walls of the Quality Inn restaurant were removed to reveal this glorious neo-Byzantine interior with its glittering gold mosaic, tunnel-vaulted ceiling by Burke & Co and walls sheathed in Tennessee and Vermont marbles.

past. The reason for the perpetuation of this myth is not hard to find. Many of the early pioneers of modernism promoted their ideas with a messianic fervour bordering on religious belief. All past styles were rejected in favour of a new form of architectural expression – modernism. Modernism was equated with modernity, and nothing else, it was argued, should be tolerated.

It is hardly surprising that the public as a whole seems bemused by all this intolerant rhetoric, which runs completely counter to burgeoning interest in the authentic restoration and adaptation of people's own homes and their interiors. Most people simply want to see the right buildings in the right places and, unlike many design professionals, have no ingrained prejudice against any particular architectural style.

In an age of architectural pluralism, surely the time has come to consign old fundamentalist attitudes to the dustbin of history, and to celebrate artistic and stylistic diversity in all its forms and traditions. Modernism is just another style, and all styles are equally valid – vernacular, classical, Gothic, Islamic, post-modern and modern.

By celebrating London's rich heritage of interiors, I hope that a more sophisticated understanding might emerge of how to manage change better and an appreciation of the extraordinary creativity of professionals from all backgrounds who produce works of art and architecture that are triumphs of individual expression. This book pays homage to the skills, imagination, craftsmanship and energy of past generations who have left their mark on London and who have not been afraid to deploy fantasy, humour, symbolism and allegory in the works they have created.

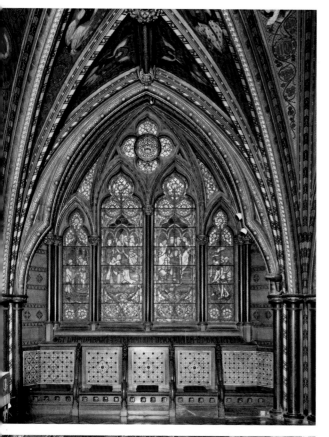

Chapel of St Mary Undercroft
Palace of Westminster

SW1A 0AA

LISTED: GRADE I

With its stupendous hammerbeam roof erected between 1394 and 1401 for Richard II, Westminster Hall is rightly celebrated as the finest timber-framed mediaeval structure in the world, but far less well known is the exquisite Chapel of St Mary Undercroft, which lies below.

St Stephen's Chapel was built as a double-storey royal chapel for Edward I in 1292-7 as a rival to La Sainte-Chapelle in Paris. Today only the former crypt, now known as the Chapel of St Mary Undercroft, survives, but it is of great architectural significance as its original master masons, Michael of Canterbury and his son, Thomas, were devotees of the complex geometrical forms in which lay the origins of the later Decorated Gothic style. Its lierne vaults, forming stellar and other patterns, are believed to be the oldest in England. The large central bosses (below left), restored by Barry after the fire of 1834, depict the martyrdoms of St Stephen, St John, St Catherine and St Laurence, and St Margaret and the Dragon. St Stephen is depicted being stoned to death by Jews dressed in the costume of the 14th century.

For a long period the chapel was used as the debating chamber of the House of Commons, but it also endured many indignities. Oliver Cromwell had the crypt whitewashed and used it as a stable for his horses, and it was also used as a coal cellar.

The internal restoration was carried out by Charles Barry's son, E M Barry, quietly over a 10-year period between 1860 and 1870 because of "rigid economic and ecclesiastical prejudice in the House of Commons", but the end result was a gorgeous, polychrome masterpiece encrusted with gold mosaics with stained glass by John Hardman Powell, an alabaster dado, and a floor of marble and Minton tiles. At the east end (top left) the windows were replaced with full-length figures of martyred saints executed by J G Crace & Son. The altar rails and gates with their kneeling angels (opposite above), designed by Barry, were modelled on the grille made in 1294 for the tomb of Eleanor of Castile in Westminster Abbey. At the west end, in a beautiful octagonal baptistery, is a huge font with an alabaster bowl, shafts of Ipplepen marble and a base of Hopton Wood stone and Purbeck marble.

Just to the east of Westminster Hall, and north of the chapel, is another of the palace's obscure treasures hidden from the public gaze: the fan-vaulted St Stephen's Cloister, rebuilt in 1526-9 at the expense of John Chamber, Henry VIII's physician, with an early Tudor Gothic courtyard at its centre, later altered by Barry, and restored again after extensive bomb damage in the Second World War.

Today the principal entrance to the undercroft is via a staircase in the south-east corner of Westminster Hall. A bomb placed here by the Fenians in 1885 was discovered by a policeman and carried into Westminster Hall, where it exploded, blew out the great window and created a large hole in the floor. At the base of the staircase leading into Old Palace Yard a plaque marks the cupboard where the suffragette Emily Wilding-Davison concealed herself for 48 hours during the 1911 census in order to record her address as the House of Commons in protest at the exclusion of women from the vote. Two years later she planted a bomb at Lloyd George's house in Surrey, causing severe damage. Shortly afterwards she was killed after stepping in front of the King's horse at the Epsom Derby.

The Supreme Court

PARLIAMENT SQUARE, SW1P 3BD

LISTED: GRADE II*

Established under the Constitutional Reform Act 2005, the Supreme Court took over the judicial functions of the Law Lords and the Judicial Committee of the Privy Council in October 2009. It is housed within the former Middlesex Guildhall on the west side of Parliament Square; a beautiful neo-Gothic building of 1911-13 designed by J G S Gibson and Peyton Skipwith, in deference to its historic neighbours, but with pronounced and innovative Art Nouveau nuances.

Faced in Portland stone with a large central tower and statuary in niches, an impressive relief frieze by the sculptor H C Fehr runs across the entrance portal, depicting scenes from English history including King John handing the Magna Carta to the barons at Runnymede, and the Duke of Northumberland handing the crown to Lady Jane Grey. Internally the building boasted the finest set of courtooms in the country and a remarkably intact Edwardian interior, which prompted SAVE Britain's Heritage to seek judicial review of the decision by Westminster City Council to grant listed building consent to make the necessary alterations.

Between 2007 and 2009 the building was adapted and converted sensitively for its new function as the Supreme Court. The entrance foyer was reconfigured with a new glazed screen and doors by Bettina Furnee, beyond which a new opening leads to the Justice's Library, crafted out of one of the former courtooms with a gallery on four sides linked to the basement below by a new staircase. As the proceedings of the Supreme Court are very different from a conventional county court, significant changes were required to Gibson's splendid courtooms, including the removal of some of the original fixed furniture and the creation of level floors, but the architectural character of the historic spaces remains, with richly modelled ceilings, panelling and stained glass. On the main staircase and the lobby to the former Council Chamber, tiled dados and historic light fittings have all been carefully conserved.

Beneath the fine hammerbeam roof in the former Middlesex Council Chamber (Court No.1), the original delicately carved bench ends by Fehr have been incorporated with great skill to terminate sets of new oak benches, and the original "throne" has been relocated to one of the galleries. The remaining original furniture from the other courtooms has been removed and stored for reuse at Snaresbrook Crown Court. A fine bust of King Edward VII by P Bryant Baker has been relocated to the basement café, while paintings and objects from the Middlesex Art Collection have been cleaned, restored and relocated around the communal areas of the building.

Designed by Feilden & Mawson, and overseen by Gilmore Hankey Kirke for the Ministry of Justice, the project demonstrates that with specialist expertise, skill and flair even the most challenging historic buildings can be adapted to new uses without sacrificing their fundamental significance and integrity. Visitors are welcome to admire the work and observe the legal proceedings when the court is open on weekdays.

At the rear of the building is one of London's little-known historical curiosities. Grimly inscribed "For such as will beg and live idle", the rusticated entrance gateway (1655) from the Old Bridewell Prison, which once stood in nearby Greencoat Row, was relocated here in 1884.

INJUSTICE ANYWHERE IS A THREAT TO JUSTICE EVERYWHERE • WE ARE CAUGHT IN AN INESCAPABLE NETWORK • MUTU

WHATEVER AFFECTS ONE DIRECTLY AFFECTS ALL INDIRECTLY • TIED IN A SINGLE GARMENT OF DESTINY

Church of St James the Less

THORNDIKE STREET SW1V 2PS

LISTED: GRADE 1

The Church of St James the Less is one of London's finest, but lesser-known, Victorian churches, and the first work in the capital by George Edmund Street, later the architect of the Royal Courts of Justice.

Built in 1859-61, it was described by Charles Eastlake as "eminently un-English". Street was well versed in Continental architecture. Each year he undertook regular architectural study tours to Europe to immerse himself in the finer points of French and Italian gothic architecture. "The best mode of improving our style is the careful study of Continental styles ... we have to go to all those lands to discover in what that development varied from our own, in what it was superior, and in what inferior".

St James the Less is heralded by its distinctive, short pyramidal spire with four corner spirelets above a high tower in the manner of an Italianate campanile. The church, which forms part of a wider complex with a school and public hall, is enclosed by elegant railings (1866) by James Leaver of Maidenhead, modelled on the screen in Barcelona Cathedral. Inside it is pure muscular Gothic, with walls of banded red and black brick structural polychromy, a floor of red and yellow glazed Maw's tiles, and short, fat granite columns with stiff-leaf carved capitals by W Pearce carrying notched and moulded brick arches. Over the font is an exuberant gilded wrought-iron canopy made by Leaver and shown at the 1862 Exhibition. The carved stone pulpit is widely regarded as one of the finest works of Thomas Earp.

The architectural climax of the interior is a wonderful sexpartite brick vault over the crossing and chancel. Above is a vast mosaic of the Last Judgement (commonly called *The Doom*) by George Frederic Watts, which replaced an earlier painted fresco of his which had deteriorated. The entire nave roof is decorated with a now sadly faded painting of the Tree of Jesse by Clayton and Bell, who also executed most of the stained-glass windows which depict the Apostles and biblical scenes.

A wall plaque commemorates Canon Arthur Thorndike, the father of the actress Dame Sybil Thorndike, who was vicar of St James's until his death during a service in 1917.

The church is surrounded by the innovative, low-rise, high-density Lillington Gardens estate, built by Westminster City Council to the designs of Darbourne and Darke from 1964 to 1970.

National Liberal Club

WHITEHALL COURT, SWIA 2HE
LISTED: GRADE II*

Renowned for its sublime romantic roofline of gables, spires and turrets, shortly after its completion in 1887 the National Liberal Club was hailed as "the most imposing clubhouse in the British metropolis"; and it was too. Not only was it the largest clubhouse ever built, until the ritzy Royal Automobile Club arrived (see pp 20-3) in 1910, it was also the first building in the capital to incorporate a lift and to be lit entirely by electricity.

The capacious club was founded by the Liberal grandee and Prime Minister W E Gladstone in 1882 to provide non-exclusive facilities for ordinary party members following the Third Reform Act, as "a home for democracy, void of the class distinctions associated with the Devonshire and Reform Clubs". G W E Russell wrote subsequently, "we never foresaw the palatial pile of terracotta and glazed tiles which now bears that name". H G Wells snorted, "The National Liberal Club is Liberalism made visible in the flesh – and Doultonware."

The architect was Alfred Waterhouse, who built a magnificent array of clubrooms behind an elevated outdoor riverside terrace, with over 140 bedrooms on the upper floors – a very early example of the use of a steel frame. The clubrooms are distinguished by the lavish use of patterned faience by Wilcock & Co in rich hues of green, yellow and brown, which impart a lustrous glow throughout the interior. This was not always appreciated. F E Smith, later the 1st Earl of Birkenhead, referred to it derisively as a useful public lavatory halfway between the Temple and Westminster. It was requisitioned for use by Canadian Army officers in the First World War. As part of the post–war refurbishments a rather swish electric escalator was installed to convey wine from the cellars to the dining room.

On 11 May 1941 the club received a direct hit from a German bomb, which destroyed the original main staircase. It was reconstructed in 1950-1 by Clyde Young and Bernard Engle as a splendid marble cantilevered oval staircase spiralling three storeys up through the building.

In 1986 the adjacent Royal Horseguards Hotel took over the bedrooms, two vast opulent ballrooms and the old Gladstone Library, the books having been sold to the University of Bristol.

The club's wine cellar was adapted from a trench dug in 1865 for the world's first underground pneumatic tube railway from Great Scotland Yard to Waterloo. The putative Whitehall–Waterloo railway was abandoned three years later and the trench modified by the club for its present use.

Beefsteak Club

9 IRVING STREET, WC2 7AH
UNLISTED

Since the 18th century there has been a long gastronomic tradition of private gentlemen's dining clubs in London, many with a reputation for quaint eccentricity. Within the august realms of clubland, the Beefsteak, and Pratt's in St James's, are two of the most exclusive. At one time, to be a member of the Beefsteak one needed to be "a relation of God – and a damned close relation at that".

There have been numerous Beefsteak Clubs, the first founded in 1705 by a group which seceded from the Kit-Kat Club. Another, the Sublime Society of Beef Steaks, followed in 1735, but was dissolved in 1867. The present club was established in 1876 as a successor to the Sublime Society. Its members hoped to rent the society's dining room at the Lyceum Theatre, but in the event took the lease on some rooms in King William IV Street above the Folly (later Toole's) Theatre. In 1882 it moved upstairs and had a vaulted ceiling constructed. When the lease expired in 1896, it moved to its current home in Irving Street and carefully copied its previous clubroom with a lofty open-timber oak roof designed by Frank Verity incorporating the club's gridiron motif.

The heart of the club is the dining room, with a long communal table for convivial dining and conversation. Previous members have included Harold Macmillan, John Betjeman, Edward Elgar, Rudyard Kipling and Edwin Lutyens.

At Pratt's, where traditionally all the staff are referred to as "George", great consternation was caused in the 1980s when a woman was recruited. The dilemma was resolved when it was decided to call her "Georgina". At the Beefsteak the steward and waiters are all called "Charles". Whilst Pratt's has a more eclectic collection of club "lumber"; including a duck-billed platypus, assorted stuffed birds and fish and the disconsolate front end of a rhinoceros, the more intellectual Beefsteak has the original gridiron rescued from the ashes of the Lyceum Theatre (the home of the Sublime Society) when it burned down, as well as a jaunty silver cockerel presented by the actor Sir Squire Bancroft.

James Smith & Sons

Hazelwood House, 53 New Oxford Street, wc1a 1bl
Listed: Grade II*

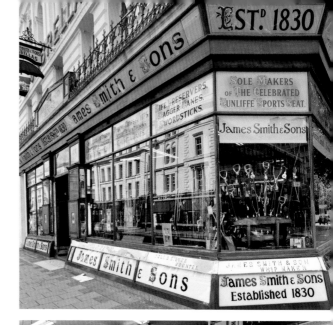

Jonas Hanway (1712-86), the traveller and philanthropist, was reputed to be the first Londoner to carry an umbrella, much to the derision of hackney coachmen, who regularly greeted him with the shout of "Frenchman, Frenchman! Why don't you call a coach?" Hanway Street, linking Oxford Street and Tottenham Court Road, is named after him. In one of those peculiar chronological resonances which reverberate through London's history, James Smith established the famous firm of umbrella makers, James Smith & Sons, a stone's throw away from Hanway Street, in Fouberts Place, off Regent Street, in 1830.

In 1857 his son, also called James, opened a shop in New Oxford Street, which had recently been laid out by Sir James Pennethorne. It was followed rapidly by six other businesses elsewhere in London, including a hatter and barbershop. From their branch in the tiny passageway at Savile Place they sold umbrellas to many of the leading figures of their day, including Lord Curzon, Gladstone and Bonar Law.

The company was one of the first to use the famous Fox steel frames, named after Samuel Fox, who created the first steel umbrella frame in 1848. In addition to umbrellas, Smith's has specialised in making canes and military swagger sticks, as well as more bespoke items such as ceremonial maces for tribal chiefs in South Africa, Nigeria and elsewhere.

Their superb shopfront and interior is a beautifully preserved example of a high-class Victorian West End shop, with cast-iron cresting to the faceted gilt and glass fascias, inscribed brass sills, elaborate black and gilt lettering to the upper panels of the windows and a splendid traditional box sign. Inside, the original mahogany counters and display cases are stocked with an array of canes, sticks and umbrellas, most of which are still manufactured in the basement.

James Smith & Sons is the largest and oldest umbrella shop in Europe, and its shopfront and interior one of the landmarks of central London.

James J Fox / Robert Lewis

19 St James's Street, sw1a 1es
Unlisted

"Robert Lewis is the most beautiful cigar shop, barring none – in London or elsewhere … The odour of Havanas is overpowering to the heathen but myrrh and mirth to the initiated. If I had to live in a shop I would dwell in Robert Lewis forever"

(G Cabrera Infante, *Holy Smoke*)

James J Fox is claimed to be the longest-established cigar merchant in Britain. Located behind an elegant, angled oak shopfront in the heart of St James's, it is the place of pilgrimage for aficionados of the cigaresque.

The firm was founded as a stockist of snuff, pipes, pouches, vestas and other smoking sundries by Christopher Lewis at 14 Long Acre in 1787. "Tobacco wrapped in a leaf" was brought back to England by troops returning from the Peninsular Wars and, as its popularity increased, the firm moved to Great Newport Street to capitalise on the interest. In 1855-6 Robert Joseph Lewis took over the firm and relocated to St James's Street, where he, and later his son Henry, rapidly built up a clientele drawn from a wide cross-section of British society, acquiring the first of eight royal warrants from the second son of Queen Victoria, HRH the Duke of Edinburgh, in the 1880s.

Amongst its more colourful regulars was Major Walter Clopton Wingfield, founder of Le Cordon Rouge, the inventor of musical formation bicycling and, perhaps more notably, the game of lawn tennis, which originally he called Sphairistike. Wingfield devised his own smoking mixture and gave Lewis's exclusive rights in exchange for 1lb of the mixture each month for life. Oscar Wilde was an habitué, ordering special cigarettes, on each of which he had painted the name Oscar in red letters. The original ledgers show he left a sizeable debt of £37. 17s. 3d.

For over 60 years Winston Churchill was a customer, having been introduced by his mother, who had a particular penchant for the firm's handmade, gold-tipped Alexandra Balkan cigarettes, which she smoked through an amber holder.

The shop retains all the accoutrements of a traditional tobacconist, complete with a carved wooden figure of a Red Indian and a smoking room for clients. In the basement is a fascinating museum of memorabilia including the oldest box of cigars in the world, made for the Great Exhibition of 1851, Churchill's chair, a hand-blown Bristol glass pipe of 1787, hookahs, commemorative cigar bands, Edward VIII's humidor and correspondence from well-known satisfied customers.

Now trading as James J Fox, the firm continues to offer 18 marques of Havana in over 350 different shapes and sizes. It is a measure of London's extraordinary global reach that it is the cigar capital of the world.

Royal Automobile Club

89-91 PALL MALL, SW1Y 5HS

LISTED: GRADE II*

With its own rifle range, Turkish baths and spectacular indoor swimming pool resembling some exotic set from a Cecil B DeMille epic, the Royal Automobile Club was the last and grandest expression of the great age of club building. Its flamboyant French façade in the style of Louis XIV is unlike any of the other gentlemen's clubs, which took their architectural inspiration from Grecian antiquity, or the elegant palazzi of Rome and Venice. This is hardly surprising as the architects were Mewès and Davis, who designed the Ritz, and Francophilia was at its height in the wake of the Entente Cordiale.

The Automobile Club of Great Britain and Ireland was founded in 1897 by Frederick Richard Simms as "a Society of Encouragement for the motoring movement and the motor and allied industries in the British Empire". After temporary sojourns at Whitehall Court and 119 Piccadilly, in 1907 it became the Royal Automobile Club under the patronage of Edward VII. A year later it acquired the site of the old War Office at Cumberland House, Pall Mall, designed by Matthew Brettingham, in a deal with the Commissioners of Woods and Forests, which stipulated that the new buildings should cost not less than £100,000. What arose cost £250,000, and an army of French craftsmen, sculptors and blacksmiths crossed the Channel to impart an authentic Parisian quality to the entire building in *la grande manière*.

Carved into the pediment over the front entrance is an allegorical sculpture of *Science as the Inspiration of the Allied Trades* by Ferdinand Faivre, complete with a primitive motor car. The wrought-iron gates and lamps are by Maison Vian of Paris.

Inside is a vision of Edwardian opulence with a massive top-lit oval vestibule in Louis XV style lined in French stuc and surrounded by a gallery at first floor level.

Immediately beyond, overlooking the garden on the south front, is the former lounge (now a restaurant) decorated by Boulanger with a sky-painted ceiling, and a stage and musicians' gallery at opposing ends. The members' dining room is in the style of Sir William Chambers, and the billiard room based on an Adam ceiling from the old War Office. To the west the great smoking room (above) by Lenygon and Morant runs from front to back with a careful reproduction of the coffered ceiling and entablature of gryphons from Brettingham's Cumberland House. The corresponding room on the east side by M Remon of Paris is designed around a series of cut-up landscape paintings attributed to Jurriaan Andriessen, taken from an old chateau in the Midi.

In the basement, lit by torchères, is the famous Byzantine swimming pool overlooked from a niche on the stair by a fine bronze sculpture of a sea goddess by Gilbert Bayes, 1927. The 90,000-gallon concrete tank, lined with Sicilian marble, is surrounded by a peristyle with pairs of massive Doric columns covered in shimmering blue and gold mosaics.

The statue of Queen Victoria was unveiled by the Kaiser during a visit with his brother Prince Henry of Prussia. To commemorate the "first aerial looping the loop by Gustav Hamel and A V Hucks" an eccentric dinner was held at which everything was eaten in reverse, starting with liqueurs and coffee and ending with hors d'oeuvres. During the war Prince Olav of Norway, General Sikorski and General de Gaulle were all regulars, and it was at the RAC that the treacherous Burgess and Maclean had their last lunch together, in May 1951, before defecting to Moscow, the choice of club made, ironically, because the Reform was full.

Middlesex Hospital Chapel

NASSAU STREET, WIT 4AA

LISTED: GRADE II*

Marooned at the centre of the vast Middlesex Hospital site, lying isolated, exposed and vulnerable, is one of the finest chapels in Britain; its future frustratingly unresolved.

The spectacular chapel of the former Middlesex Hospital was designed by John Loughborough Pearson and begun in 1891, although it was not completed until 1930 by his son, Frank. Built as a memorial to Major Alexander Ross MP, a chairman of the Board of Governors, funding was provided by his family for a lavishly decorated interior in a rich eclectic mixture of Italianate, Byzantine and neo-Romanesque styles.

Pearson returned from a study tour of Italy in 1874 as a passionate enthusiast for the elaborate polychrome pavements of mediaeval Italian churches, which later he deployed to great effect in his own work.

At the Middlesex Hospital the chancel floor is a sumptuous juxtaposition of green, yellow and black marble Cosmati work complemented by green onyx slabs to the walls of the nave and sanctuary. Above is a band of chevron-patterned marble and rich mosaic work. Soaring overhead, the groin-vaulted ceilings shimmer with gold mosaics and blue stars in a stunning display of craftsmanship by Robert Davison, whose Decorative Arts Studio was in nearby Marylebone. To complement his unified vision for the interior, for the stained glass Pearson turned to his favourite artists, Clayton & Bell.

On his death in December 1899, Pearson's son Frank took over, completing the last two bays of the gold mosaic ceiling with icons of the Apostles either side of the sacred monogram IHC. With the reconstruction of the hospital in 1929, additional space was created to form a narrow baptistery which Frank Pearson embellished in full-blown Byzantine style with a lapis-lazuli dome and angels bearing scrolls.

In 1936 Rudyard Kipling lay in state here. Until its closure in 2005, the chapel provided daily solace for many at their hour of greatest need.

Queen's Chapel

MARLBOROUGH ROAD, SWIA IDH

LISTED: GRADE I

The Queen's Chapel was once an integral part of the St James's Palace complex, until 1809 when the connecting buildings burned down. In 1856-7 Marlborough Road was created, severing the chapel from the palace.

The Queen's Chapel is one of the glories of English Renaissance architecture: the first church in England to be built in a wholly classical style, and one of the best surviving works of Inigo Jones. It was built by James I for his son Charles as a Catholic chapel in 1623 and completed two years later for use by his French queen, Henrietta Maria.

Externally it is a plain, pedimented brick box faced in render with Portland stone quoins and dressings. At the east end the broad Venetian window with square Corinthian columns is believed to be the earliest to survive in the country.

The interior is exceptionally fine, with an elliptical painted and gilded coffered vault in timber rather than plaster, modelled on Palladio's Temple of Venus and Rome. The furnishings are principally later, following modifications carried out for Catherine of Braganza in 1662, 1679-80 and later by Wren in 1682-4. However, the Royal Pew in the West Gallery (top right), with its large hybrid chimneypiece with segmental half-pediments and festoons, is part of Jones's original decorative scheme. The reredos with its quadrant wings of 1682-4 is by Grinling Gibbons, although the pedimented centrepiece containing a 17th century altarpiece of the Holy Family by Annibale, or possibly Agostino Carracci, is from the Royal Collection. Overhead the Stuart and Portuguese royal arms are framed by gilded angels and festoons. The balustraded altar rails were given by Queen Anne in 1702.

Lancaster House

STABLE YARD, ST JAMES'S, SW1A 1BB

LISTED: GRADE I

A palace is not merely a large house, but a building specifically designed for formal ceremony with a sequential progression of spaces and features intended to impress upon the visitor the wealth and status of its owner. Lancaster House has been described as "the only true private palace ever built in London". Originally known as York House (1825-7), subsequently as Stafford House (1827-1914), and now as Lancaster House, it has had a chequered history.

Construction began in 1825 for the Duke of York and Albany – "the Grand Old Duke of York" – initially to designs by Sir Robert Smirke, but the headstrong duke soon sacked his architect and appointed Benjamin Dean Wyatt in his place. When the spendthrift duke died in a sea of debt in 1827, the unfinished shell of the house was sold to one of the wealthiest men in England, the Marquess of Stafford (later 1st Duke of Sutherland), whose eldest son brought it to fruition, adding a rather cumbersome attic storey in 1833-6 to Smirke's design.

Situated in a large private garden adjacent to the Green Park and facing St James's Park, externally its Bath stone elevations are understated, but the opulent interiors are staggering, prompting Queen Victoria to remark to her friend Harriet, the 2nd Duchess, "I have come from my house to your palace." Lavishly designed in the style of Louis XIV, the interiors are a melding of the work of Benjamin Dean Wyatt, Sir Robert Smirke and Sir Charles Barry.

The colossal entrance hall and staircase lit by an oblong lantern is lined in yellow and black scagliola with inset paintings of 1841-8 by G G Lorenzi in the manner of Paolo Veronese. The intricate cast-iron staircase balustrade is by J Bramah & Sons.

At first floor level the Music Room has a circle-coffered ceiling with borders derived from Palmyra (left). Beyond, the vast Picture Gallery (left above), also with Palmyrene decoration, once held the Sutherlands' magnificent art collection in "the most magnificent room in London" with works by the great European masters including Van Dyck, Rembrandt, Rubens, Titian and Murillo. In the lantern is Guercino's painting of *St Chrisogonus Borne by Angels* (1622) taken from Rome (opposite below left). Between two recesses with carved lunettes is a grandiloquent green marble chimneypiece by Crozatier of Paris, lavishly ornamented with gold caryatids beneath a gilded overmantel and sumptuous French clock (opposite below middle). Over the north-east Ante Room is a fine 16th century painting of the *Three Graces* attributed to Battista Zelotti (left below). Another superb chimneypiece (c1837) by Richard Westmacott Jr, with children representing winter and autumn, can be found in the Green Room, which was once the boudoir of the 2nd Duchess. Unusually there are more fine state rooms at ground floor level, including the splendid State Dining Room (1828-9) (opposite below right).

As liberals and patrons of the arts, the Sutherlands received a galaxy of 19th century celebrities at the house, including the social reformer Lord Shaftesbury, the anti-slavery campaigner Harriet Beecher Stowe and the Italian revolutionary Giuseppe Garibaldi, whose stay in April 1864 is commemorated by a roundel by Luigi Fabbrucci unveiled 20 years later.

In 1912 the house was purchased by Sir William Lever (later 1st Lord Leverhulme), the Lancastrian soap magnate, who promptly presented it to the nation. Between the wars it was the home of the London Museum, but in 1950 it was taken over by the Foreign Office for receptions and international conferences.

The Queen's coronation banquet was held here in 1952. Subsequently it was the venue for several conferences to settle the future of various colonies of the British Empire including Malaya in 1956, Nigeria in 1957-8, Kenya in 1960, 1962 and 1963 and, most famously, the independence of Southern Rhodesia as Zimbabwe, through the Lancaster House Agreement of 1979.

The Wolseley

160 PICCADILLY, W1J 9EB

LISTED: GRADE II*

The Wolseley is now in its third incarnation, having been built in 1921 as a prestigious West End showroom for Wolseley cars. Set within the ground floor of a monumental classical building designed by William Curtis Green, the lavish vaulted Florentine interior and exquisite Chinese lacquer work provided a sumptuous upmarket setting for the swanky marque. The cars were displayed on the black and white marble floor with its centrepiece of radiating black and white stars. However, as early as October 1926 the venture had failed, and the company went into receivership with debts of £2m.

The building was sold to Barclays Bank, who promptly recalled Curtis Green to convert the building into a sumptuous new banking hall, which opened in April 1927, and which reflected the commercial might of one of the "big five" British banks.

Barclays had never adopted a coherent house style. The commissioning of new banks was left to local managers, who were given considerable latitude, and, doubtless in the interests of economy, at Piccadilly the interior was adapted to reinforce the exotic Chinese theme which had been executed by Walter Brierley. The panelled counters were crafted in black and red lacquer with Chinese motifs, and bespoke furniture designed by Curtis Green included black cane and lacquer work chairs, a Chinese chest, a post box and stamp machine.

The 1920s were the heyday of British commercial influence in the treaty ports of China – Shanghai, Hong Kong and Canton. Chinese design filtered back and was seen, albeit briefly, as a modish expression of Britain's global wealth and power. The nearby contemporaneous shopfronts of Jackson's of Piccadilly, tea merchants, which still survive albeit in new uses, have pagoda-style tops adorned with Chinese figures.

In 1999 Barclays closed, and the interior was converted with great sensitivity into the Wolseley restaurant by David Collins, architects, reopening in November 2003.

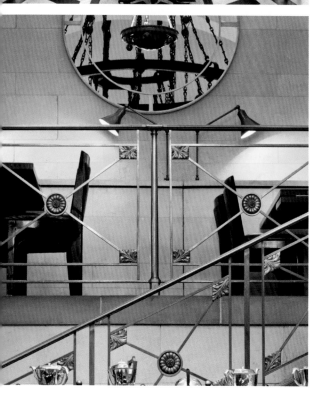

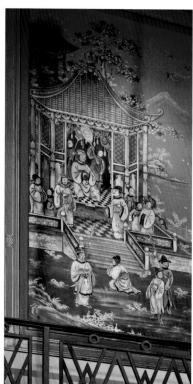

Park Lane Hotel

PICCADILLY, W1J 7BX

LISTED: GRADE II

O verlooking Green Park and faced in white Burmantoft "Marmo" faience, externally the Park Lane Hotel is a rather incoherent composition, with a deeply recessed centre and black columns to the entrances, but the interior is a complete revelation.

Beyond the main entrance the restaurant in the west wing has reset panelling and boiseries in Louis XV style, designed in 1904 by Carlhian and Beaumetz of Paris for the American financier Pierpoint Morgan's house in Princes Gate, Kensington. To the east, the Oak Room is a copy of the Globe Room of 1637 from the Reindeer Hotel in Banbury, but these are a mere prelude to the amazing 1920s Silver Gallery, staircase and ballroom, which form the largest and most sumptuous unbroken sequence of Art Deco spaces in London.

Designed by Kenneth Anns and Henry Tanner in 1927, the rooms are approached through a separate entrance from Piccadilly. The large entrance hall, or Silver Gallery, in pink mauve and silver hues is breathtaking. Clustered vertical tubes of light frame the entrances beside arched mirrors in silver gilt frames. The staircases beyond are marked by triple-tiered, annular lights which form exotic capitals to the silver gilt columns beneath. Glowing cylindrical stairlights match the geometrical brass handrails.

On the staircase walls are paintings by a Miss Gilbert. One depicts stylised classical female figures, daringly topless, but striking the carefree poses of giddy young flappers of the 1920s – all in silver leaf lacquered to the walls in gold. Another symbolically depicts nymphs with wild beasts. The staircases lead down to a gallery overlooking a huge basement ballroom finished by Higgs and Hill with wall panelling enriched with winged horses and youths, pink-tinted shaped mirrors, fountain wall-lights, frosted-glass chandeliers and palmette-decorated plasterwork. Surrounding rooms, lavatories and their details in full period style are all part of the total aesthetic experience. It is sensational.

Here in the Jazz Age London's *jeunesse dorée* would trip the light fantastic to the Charleston, shimmy and Black Bottom. With characteristic bobbed hair, "the badge of flapperhood", frivolous flappers would "trot like foxes, limp like lame ducks, one-step like cripples, and all to the bizarre yawp of strange instruments". Freed from the constraints of stays and corsets, and dressed like boys with flattened chests, etiolated young women flaunted their sexuality, scandalising their elders and ushering in the age of the new, "modern" woman.

Clermont Club

44 BERKELEY SQUARE, WIJ 5AR

LISTED: GRADE I

In 1696 the 3rd Lord Berkeley of Stratton sold his house in Piccadilly to the Duke of Devonshire with an explicit undertaking not to allow buildings north of its gardens, a commitment which was honoured for almost 200 years. The result was a continuous sweep of open landscape from Berkeley House, through the gardens of Lansdowne House (built in the 1760s) and on through the central gardens of Berkeley Square to the edge of the Grosvenor Estate beyond.

In 1738-9 a group of large houses was erected on the eastern side of the square, followed immediately by an even more opulent group on the west side. Of these, No 44, now the Clermont Club, is widely regarded as the finest terrace house in London. It was designed by the elderly William Kent for Lady Isabella Finch, the 7th daughter of the 7th Earl of Winchelsea, known as Don Dismal for his swarthy appearance. Bel, as she was called, was a middle-aged spinster and maid of honour to Princesses Amelia and Caroline, daughters of George II.

The reticent brick exterior and large rusticated arched entrance give little clue to the splendours which lie inside. Beyond the plain, stone-flagged entrance hall and tiny former porter's lodge is the dramatic centrepiece of the whole house – a staircase which has no equal in Palladian architecture and which was widely admired by contemporaries. Horace Walpole described it: "as beautiful as a piece of scenery, and considering the space, of art as can be imagined!"

It was revolutionary. There had never been anything like it. At a time when staircases conventionally were either square or spiral, Kent produced a highly complex series of interpenetrating spaces: an exercise in pure theatre, creating the illusion of a palatial interior within the confines of a terrace house. The curved flights of stairs break back in on themselves to a bridge across the first floor landing and a screen of Ionic columns, behind which the stair rises to the second floor. Above is a coffered dome reminiscent of Santa Maria Maggiore in Rome. The scrolled ironwork resembling seahorses evokes Kent's earlier work at Holkham Hall.

The staircase is but a precursor to one of the finest rooms in London, the Saloon or Great Chamber, with a coved and coffered gilded geometrical ceiling inset with grisaille paintings on blue and red grounds, depicting the *Loves of the Gods*, probably painted by Kent himself before his death in 1748. At each end are matching fireplaces by Joseph Pickford surmounted by pier glasses and trophies, the walls lined with dark blue damask introduced as part of John Fowler's restoration for the Clermont Club in 1962.

Behind the Saloon is Lady Bel's bedroom and boudoir, remodelled by Henry Holland in 1790 after the house was sold to Lord Clermont following her death in 1771. Lady Clermont, a friend of Marie Antoinette, was an ardent Francophile, which accounts for the stylistic change. Sympathetic restoration and alterations were carried out by John Fowler and Philip Jebb between 1962 and 1964, including the octagonal Gothick garden pavilion.

From 1962 the Clermont Club was the haunt of a wealthy group of buccaneering British gamblers including five dukes, five marquesses, nearly 20 earls and two cabinet ministers, alongside such luminaries as Ian Fleming, Lucien Freud, James Goldsmith and Lord Lucan. In the basement is Annabel's, the private members' restaurant and nightclub.

Geo F Trumper

9 CURZON STREET, WIJ 5HQ

UNLISTED

Geo F Trumper is that rare commodity – a surviving example of a traditional gentlemen's barbershop with a beautifully presented period interior, complete with individual mahogany cubicles and glass display cases from the early 20th century full of fragrant scents bearing the names of great British figures: Marlborough, Wellington and Curzon among others.

George F Trumper opened his first barbershop in Curzon Street in 1875, although the present handsome, stone-faced building was not erected until later, c1912. The plain polished oak shopfront with its black and gilt lettering on the windows and sill boards epitomises the understated urbane elegance of old Mayfair. Given the aristocratic and military clientele he attracted, Trumper made his shop feel like more a luxurious gentlemen's club than just a functional barber's shop, an ambience which continues to this day.

Inside, the individual private cubicles are divided by glazed mahogany screens with dark red velvet curtains; the walls lined with hunting scenes and shelves of the firm's world-famous colognes, grooming products and shaving accessories. Beneath the display cases is a dado lined with plush studded green leather.

Criterion Restaurant and Theatre

224 Piccadilly, w1j 9hp
Listed: Grade II*

In 1871 the railway caterers Spiers & Pond held a competition for the design of a new entertainments complex comprising a restaurant, dining rooms, smoking room, grand hall and theatre for a site on the south side of Piccadilly Circus occupied by an old galleried coaching inn, The White Bear. Thomas Verity was selected as architect. The complex was the first of a new generation of monster restaurants catering for the newly affluent middle classes. Designed in French Second Empire style and influenced by Charles Garnier's work in Paris, it opened in 1874 and was an instant success. Eight years later it was extended by Verity's son, Frank.

Beneath the huge restaurant, which catered for over 2,000 diners, is "an underground temple of drama" – the Criterion Theatre, which Verity modelled on the Athenée in Paris. This was made possible by modern services such as lifts and mechanical ventilation, and fireproof separation from the restaurant above. The theatre entrance (top right) retains its original appearance with a painted ceiling, mirrors and tiles made by W B Simpson & Son and cartoon figures by A S Coke. Critics claimed that "the effect would be like a butcher's shop" but, having experimented with tiling at the Mansion House Station Restaurant, the clients were determined to adopt it. Verity concluded that it was "bright and clean, practically indestructible, and not too expensive, and what is more important, it will wash".

The theatre was given an illusion of space by the clever use of mirrors and decoration, although shortly after its opening a young actress, Violet Vanbrugh, described acting there as being "something like an isolated race of submerged beings from one of H G Wells' imaginative novels".

To the left of the main entrance is the former buffet area, known as the Long Bar, now the Criterion Restaurant. In 1899 this was extended to include a raised smoking room to the rear (opposite top left). At the same time the interior was remodelled by Frank Verity to form a spectacular neo-Byzantine "Marble Restaurant" resembling an Aladdin's cave. Beneath a glittering gold mosaic, tunnel-vaulted ceiling by Burke & Co are walls sheathed in Tennessee and Vermont marbles, their first use in England. By 1980 the interior was believed to be no longer intact, but in 1983 it was rediscovered beneath the Formica-covered walls of the Quality Inn. I recall well the thrill of its rediscovery on removing some of the ceiling panels and finding the hidden splendours beneath, and the subsequent battle to prevent the demolition of the jewel-like smoking room at the rear. The entire interior was restored with great aplomb in 1984.

It was at the original Long Bar in the Criterion that Conan Doyle imagined the meeting between Sherlock Holmes and Dr Watson.

Algerian Coffee Stores

52 OLD COMPTON STREET, W1D 4PB
UNLISTED

A great city can be measured by the quality and extent of its historic shops and cafés, which coalesce to confer a very distinctive sense of place. At a time when so many high streets are under siege from clone stores and corporate chains, it is doubly important to ensure that those that remain are safeguarded and cherished. Unlike Paris, in London historic shops and uses are at the mercy of market forces and not accorded preferential business rates.

Established in 1887, the Algerian Coffee Stores is one of those delightful specialist shops that make London such a rich and diverse world city. Behind its distinctive pillar-box-red shopfront in the heart of Soho, many of the original late 19th century fittings survive including the mahogany counter, display cases and shelves.

The shop is permeated with the pungent aromas of over 80 different coffees from across the globe and more than 120 exotic teas with wildly romantic names – Silver Snail, Rose Congou and, best of all, Dragon's Whiskers.

London has still not produced an effective mechanism for protecting historic shops and uses for the benefit of future generations.

W Sitch & Co

48 Berwick Street, w1f 8jd

Listed: Grade II

The historic terrace houses of 18th and 19th century London are immensely adaptable and capable of accommodating a multitude of different uses from housing, offices and commercial space to public houses, clubs and workshops. As a result many light industries and craft workshops in central and inner London can still be found in what were once elegant Georgian and Regency houses.

W Sitch & Co, art metal and lighting specialists, is a wonderfully atmospheric example. Founded in 1776, the year of the Declaration of American Independence, it has been located in an early 19th century town house in Soho since 1903, and specialises in the restoration, renovation and replication of historic lighting and fittings from any period.

Every surface of the interior of the building is crammed with light fittings, lamps and specialist metalwork. A fine early 18th century staircase with turned balusters and ancient timber treads worn smooth by the passage of time leads to a veritable treasure trove. The upper floors are lined with a bewildering array of sconces, wall lights, chandeliers, lanterns, lamps and candelabra in a plethora of designs and styles. At the rear is a fully operational workshop and forge for the manufacture and polishing of individual artefacts. The basement resembles a burial crypt – piled high with metalwork, fixtures, fittings and accessories.

Amongst the company's august clientele are the National Trust, English Heritage and 10 Downing Street.

Petrie Museum of Egyptian Archaeology

MALET PLACE, WCIE 6BT

UNLISTED

Housed above a set of 19th century stables, the Petrie Museum of Egyptian Archaeology is one of London's most captivating hidden gems; a veritable treasure trove of over 80,000 objects which comprise one of the world's finest, and little-known, collections of Ancient Egyptian and Sudanese artefacts.

Much of the initial collection was donated by the writer Amelia Edwards, who in 1882 co-founded the Egypt Exploration Fund, dedicated to the research and preservation of Egyptian ancient monuments. On her death in 1892 she bequeathed her library and collection of antiquities to University College, London, and endowed the Edwards Chair of Egyptology, the first to be established in Britain. The first Edwards Professor was (Sir) William Flinders Petrie (1853-1942), one of the titans of early Egyptology, who excavated many of the most important Egyptian sites including Tanis, Abydos and Amarna, the city founded by the monotheistic Pharaoh Akhenaten.

Petrie's collection was arranged in galleries and intended primarily for reference by scholars, students and academics rather than the public. After his retirement in 1933, his successors added to it extensively. In the early 1950s it was recovered from wartime storage and moved into its current home in Malet Place, adjacent to the Science Library of University College.

Petrie was notorious for his extreme right-wing views and was an ardent believer in eugenics. On his death in Jerusalem in 1942 his body was buried in the Protestant Cemetery of Mt Zion, but rather conceitedly he bequeathed his head to the Royal College of Surgeons, so it could be studied for its intellectual capacity. Unfortunately it went AWOL, and was only discovered in London many years later.

The collection is full of some of the oldest Egyptian artefacts and many 'firsts', including the earliest example of worked metal, the first worked iron beads, the earliest example of glazing, the oldest wills on papyrus and one of the earliest fragments of linen along with a beadnet dress of a dancer from 2400BC, a suit of armour from the royal palace at Memphis and the world's largest collection of Roman mummy portraits from the first and second centuries AD.

UC.14334.

Moulds, for shaping inlays, amulets and seals to be glazed; threading holes were added to these for necklaces.

Red clay mould of woman's head. Tell el Amarna, pl.XVII, 176 Samson, Amarna, p.96, pl.50.

St Christopher's Chapel
Hospital for Sick Children

GREAT ORMOND STREET, WC1N 3JH

LISTED: GRADE II*

Dedicated to St Christopher, the patron saint of children, the chapel at the Hospital for Sick Children is not only profoundly moving, but also one of London's most unexpected and beautiful interiors.

The exquisite interior, resembling a mediaeval jewelled reliquary, was designed by Edward Middleton Barry in memory of his sister-in-law, Caroline, the wife of William Henry Barry, the eldest son of Sir Charles Barry, who with Pugin co-designed the Palace of Westminster. On her death her husband donated the staggering sum of £40,000 for the chapel, with a stipend for the chaplain to cater for the spiritual needs of impoverished children from the surrounding slums.

Unveiled in 1875, the tiny neo-Byzantine chapel was designed to inculcate Christian faith and religious awe in children who could not read through vibrant polychrome detail and the use of spiritual iconography. "We cannot regret the expenditure, as one thinks how the little ones will revel in the beauty," wrote a contemporary observer in *Christian World*.

The central dome is painted with an orchestra of 12 angels, each playing musical instruments, at the centre of which is the Christian symbol of a pelican plucking blood from her breast to feed her young – an allegory of Christ shedding his blood for humanity.

On the north wall is a heart-rending mural of children from all historical periods called to Christ above the quotation "Suffer the little children to come unto me". Opposite, on the south wall, Jesus instructs his disciples to "Feed my lambs. Feed my sheep." Below are poignant short rows of black ebonised pews designed for children.

The columns of rare pink Devonshire marble carrying the central dome are carved with gilded flowers, owls, squirrels and mythical beasts designed to captivate and stimulate children's imaginations. The sanctuary is divided from the nave by a rich marble screen with brass gates inlaid with glowing coloured glass ornament. Beyond, the ceiling of the apse shimmers with gold stars against a dark blue sky above eight intertwined angels depicting the Christian values – faith, truth, patience, purity, obedience, charity, honour and hope – over rich stained-glass windows by Clayton & Bell illustrating the boyhood of Christ. The elaborate Cosmati work floor is by Antonio Salviati and allegedly modelled on a pavement in St Mark's, Venice.

In 1992 the chapel was relocated from its original position on the first floor of the hospital in one of the most audacious exercises ever undertaken in conservation engineering. After underpinning on an enormous concrete raft, the chapel was moved inch by inch using greased slides and hydraulic rams into its current position, where it was reopened as part of a complex of new hospital buildings by the late Diana, Princess of Wales on St Valentine's Day, 1994.

New Hall and Library
Lincoln's Inn

WC2A 3TL

LISTED: GRADE II*

By the early 19th century membership of Lincoln's Inn had expanded so much that the Benchers resolved to build a whole new range of facilities. The result was a dramatic new complex of wonderfully romantic neo-Tudor buildings soaring above the boundary walls to Lincoln's Inn Fields – complementing and enhancing the adjacent 17th and 18th century collegiate courtyards of the older parts of the Inn.

The New Hall and Library were designed by Philip Hardwick in 1842 and completed by his son, Philip Charles, in 1845. John Loughborough Pearson oversaw much of the detail, which was executed in bright red diapered brick with stone dressings to echo the character and texture of the oldest part of the Inn. A huge central lantern breaks the roofline to reinforce its romantic external skyline of crenellations and towers. Seen in conjunction with the spires of Street's Royal Courts of Justice beyond, it is one of the most sublime views in London.

The interiors are breathtaking. The Hall is over 60ft high with a false hammerbeam roof, which is actually hung from metal rods with painted pendant beam ends. Commanding the entire hall is a huge fresco of *The Lawgivers* (1852-3) by George Frederick Watts, featuring the great lawmakers of history from Moses and Muhammad to Edward I and Charlemagne. The walls are panelled and carry the arms and portraits of past Benchers and grandees.

A lofty octagonal lantern links the Hall with the Library, which is rightly considered to be one of the most beautiful in the world – a phalanx of bookcases and iron galleries dividing the spaces into bays under another superb hammerbeam roof, all lit by great Perpendicular stained-glass windows in canted bays at each end of the L-shaped space; the original library having been extended by George Gilbert Scott in 1871-3, who reused Hardwick's original east window. At the centre of the space stands a statue of Lord Erskine (1830) by Westmacott. With over 80,000 books, it holds one of the world's oldest collections on law and jurisprudence.

Hardwick's work at Lincoln's Inn, and Scott's sensitive later extensions, are an eloquent demonstration of how an understanding of context and a mastery of style can create new buildings for new generations which enhance rather than diminish local character and a sense of place.

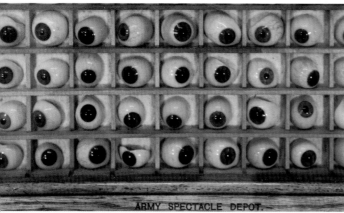

ARMY SPECTACLE DEPOT.

British Optical Association Museum

41-42 CRAVEN STREET, WC2N 5NG

LISTED: NO 41 – GRADE II

Founded in 1901 by the optician J H Sutcliffe (1867-1941), the British Optical Association Museum is now hosted by the College of Optometrists, after a peripatetic existence over the past 100 years.

It was first opened to the public in 1914 at Clifford's Inn Hall, prompted by Sutcliffe's desire to establish "An Optical House Beautiful" in line with the fashionable concepts of the Aesthetic Movement. Later it moved to Brook Street and then to Earl's Court before arriving at its current location in 1997, a fine early Georgian house built c1730, with a replica extension erected in 1988. Sutcliffe's legacy is a quirky collection of over 18,000 items relating to ophthalmic optics, the human eye and visual aids, as well as archival material, paintings and prints.

The Print Room is covered with portraits, prints and paintings all on an ophthalmic theme, including the first illustration of a pair of swimming goggles in a print of 1590. Amongst the allegorical pictures and satires by Stradanus, Cruikshank and Gillray is a caricature depicting a revolving top hat with assorted pairs of glasses suspended from the brim. On the end wall is an oil painting of St Lucia, the patron saint of those suffering from eye diseases, traditionally depicted holding her eyes on a golden plate. At the rear is the college's collection of oil paintings, including a 16th century portrait of St Jerome in his study with spectacles, a rare 17th century Venetian canvas with the sitter wearing glasses, and a fine portrait of Benjamin Franklin, who lived nearby at 36 Craven Street.

The museum display is a fascinating juxtaposition of old and new objects, including the spectacles of famous personalities from Dr Johnson to Ronnie Corbett, and the sides of Dr Crippen's glasses, the lenses missing after he tried to use them to cut his own throat in prison in a failed suicide attempt. The cabinets house an extensive collection of porcelain eyebaths, binoculars, spyglasses and jealousy glasses with sideways mirrors to allow the owner to discreetly eye up potential suitors. Look for the dark adaptation goggles with red lenses used by Second World War pilots to adjust their night vision prior to take off, and the early revolving self-service cabinet of spectacles (1889) made by the Automatic Sight Testing and Optical Supply Co Ltd.

The real highlights are the trays of glass eyes, one of which (not for the faint-hearted) has 160 models of diseases and ocular malformations. Another is a selection used as ocular prostheses for troops during the First World War. Alongside artificial eyes from Ancient Egypt to allow the dead to see into the next life is the earliest British contact lens (1933), and an alien Long-Necked Jedi eye from *Star Wars – The Attack of the Clones* (2002).

The Sherlock Holmes

10-11 NORTHUMBERLAND STREET, WC2N 5DB
UNLISTED

Only three British characters from fiction have achieved universal renown – Sherlock Holmes, James Bond and Harry Potter. Such is the reputation of Sherlock Holmes and the evocative appeal of Victorian and Edwardian London that overseas many believe he actually existed. This is perhaps understandable, as a complete recreation of his lodgings was built by Marylebone Borough Library and the Abbey National Building Society for the Festival of Britain in 1951, and subsequently it went on a world tour. In 1957 the entire exhibit was acquired by Whitbread & Co, who installed it in The Northumberland Arms (designed by J W Brooker in 1891) and rechristened the pub after the great sleuth.

The Northumberland Hotel featured in several stories. It was here that Sir Hugo Baskerville lost his boot before leaving for Dartmoor, while Holmes and Watson frequented the adjacent Turkish baths, the old entrance to which can still be discerned in Craven Passage to the side of the pub.

The pub is strewn with original cartoons, newspaper cuttings, film stills and memorabilia, including Dr Watson's old service revolver and a distinctly tacky but lugubrious stuffed head of the Hound of the Baskervilles. In the restaurant on the upper floor is a complete, if rather dog-eared, replica of Holmes and Watson's sitting room and study set behind a glass partition; all as conceived in 1957. Here is the portrait of General Gordon, although the "veritable gasogene" seems to have vanished. To add to the authenticity, the wall is peppered with revolver shots marking out the royal insignia "VR".

In 1990 the number 221b Baker Street was assigned to the much more convincing Sherlock Holmes Museum in Baker Street which opened in the same year. A year later another opened in the basement of the old English church in Meiringen, Switzerland, the village where Holmes stayed before his fateful encounter with Professor Moriarty at the Reichenbach Falls.

"They still live for all that love them well; in a romantic chamber of the heart, in a nostalgic country of the mind; where it is always 1895." (Vincent Starrett)

Australian High Commission

AUSTRALIA HOUSE, STRAND, WC2B 4LA

LISTED: GRADE II

Built between 1913 and 1918 on a huge triangular site created by the Holborn to Strand improvement scheme, Australia House was the outcome of an architectural competition won by the Scots architects A Marshal Mackenzie & Son. Judged unanimously to be "a lasting monument to the importance of the Commonwealth and a splendid addition to the architecture of London", the splayed corner was enriched in 1924 with a magnificent bronze sculpture of Phoebus and the horses of the sun by the eminent Australian sculptor Sir Bertram Mackennal. Adjoining the main entrance below are two huge figurative groups by a fellow Australian, Harold Parker; a powerful expression of burgeoning national pride and dominion status.

The sumptuous interior, lined with Australian marble and exotic woods, is configured around a huge central axis culminating in an aisled exhibition hall embellished with the Australian coat of arms, the six states of Australia having become a federation within the British Empire in 1902. Flanking the huge Beaux Arts entrance hall are two superb marble staircases with ironwork by Starkie Gardner, and great entrance gates designed by the Bromsgrove Guild.

At the laying of the foundation stone by King George V on 24 July 1913, "a long-drawn, plaintive cry swelled and died again and again" as the largely Australian crowd shouted, "Coo-ee." Poignantly, by the time the King officially opened the building, five years later in August 1918, over 60,000 Australians lay dead following the carnage of the First World War. A further 156,000 were wounded, gassed or taken prisoner.

Australia House is the oldest Australian diplomatic mission, and the largest continuously occupied foreign mission in London.

Lloyds Bank

222 STRAND, WC2R 1BB

LISTED: GRADE II

Today it is commonplace for the grand interiors of redundant banks to be converted into restaurants, but over 120 years ago the exact reverse occurred at the Law Courts branch of Lloyds Bank.

Since 1612 the site had been occupied by the Palsgrave Tavern, a favourite haunt of the playwright Ben Jonson. It took its name from Frederick Palsgrave, later the King of Bohemia, who married Princess Elizabeth, the daughter of James I, but in 1883 the Jacobean tavern was demolished for the "Royal Courts of Justice Restaurant" designed by Goymour Cuthbert and William Wimble, the architect of the Baltic Exchange. Three years later, having failed to attract lawyers and their clients from the Royal Courts directly opposite, it closed. It was then followed by the Palsgrave Restaurant, but that too was short-lived, and the building remained unoccupied until 1895, when it was taken over and converted from a restaurant into Lloyds Bank.

The branch was the result of an amalgamation of Lloyds Ltd with bankers Messrs Praed & Co of Truro in 1891, and the subsequent merger of the two with R Twining & Co in 1895. Pistols used to protect coachmen on the long journey from Truro to London can still be seen in the senior manager's office.

Described on its opening in the *Penny Illustrated Paper* as "the handsomest and most elegant bank in London", the original restaurant interior survives. The tour de force is the lustrous entrance lobby, which can be seen from the street – a cornucopia of brown, blue and green tiles with ornamental fountains forming a centrepiece at each end. Beyond is a short lobby lined with carved American walnut and sequoia wood with capitals in the form of inscrutable owls. The roof lantern above is decorated with hand-painted tiles depicting the Palsgrave arms.

Within, the highlight of the main banking hall is a series of hand-painted Doulton tile panels depicting characters and scenes from the plays of Ben Jonson, and tile pictures of chrysanthemums, flowers and plants from the Temple Gardens show of 1892.

For all its antiquarian references, the building incorporated the latest technological advances. Fresh water was drawn from an artesian well 238ft below ground. Electric light was supplied with the assistance of steam-driven dynamos, and the whole building was air-conditioned using an ingenious system based on the ventilation of ships' holds.

There is a suggestion that the original dining room was ventilated by a pair of women riding a tandem bicycle in the basement to power a giant pair of bellows, which forced air into the ground floor. Whilst apocryphal, it may just be true. During refurbishment, a piece of equipment resembling a bicycle was found in the basement alongside a mass of ducting, which appears to be the remains of the original system.

Prudential Assurance Company Offices

HOLBORN BARS, EC1N 2NQ

LISTED: GRADE II*

The romantic serrated skyline of the former Prudential Assurance Company offices in Holborn stands as a glorious reproach to the staggeringly inept post-war buildings which surround it. The soaring complex of red brick and terracotta set around a central courtyard (now known as Waterhouse Square) resembles a university quadrangle and was built in stages over a 25-year period.

The company was founded in Hatton Garden by Edgar Horne on 30 May 1848 as the Prudential Mutual Assurance Investment and Loan Association, pioneering the sale of one-penny insurance policies to the working classes. These were collected by door-to-door salesmen – the origin of the stereotypical figure, the Man from the Pru. In 1879 it resolved to move its headquarters from Ludgate Hill to a new building at Holborn Bars.

Alfred Waterhouse was chosen for the task. His characteristic use of red brick and terracotta and romantic Gothic Revival style set a precedent for over 20 regional Prudential offices around the country. The building progressively replaced the old legal precinct of Furnival's Inn and The Old Bell Tavern, one of London's last coaching inns.

The first phase, at the junction of Brooke Street and Holborn, was completed in 1876-9. Further ranges were added in 1885-8, 1895, and 1897-1901. In 1932 the original 1879 range was rebuilt by E M Joseph in a similar style externally, but with distinctive 1930s interior including a sleek directors' washroom in a modish Art Deco style.

The front of the 1897-1901 range contains a series of lustrous interiors sheathed in Burmantoft's terracotta in a brightly coloured mixture of brown, green and yellow hues. The magnificent vaulted directors' staircase is richly embellished with Gothic trefoils and terrazzo floors in intricate geometrical patterns. The principal offices are panelled throughout with original and replicated light fittings. The galleried library with its Gothic arcaded chimneypiece, moulded plaster ceilings and original bookcases remains in library use.

The basement of the E M Joseph building included a muniment room for the safe storage of deeds and securities, entry to which was via two gigantic steel doors and a drawbridge. The two Chubb doors are preserved in their original position, although the room itself has now gone.

In the north-west corner of the courtyard is one of the most beautiful war memorials in London, dedicated to the 786 employees who died in the Great War. Sculpted in bronze by F V Blundstone in 1922, it depicts a dying soldier cradled in the arms of two winged angels. Originally sited on the central axis beneath the huge carriage entrance, it was relocated in 1993 as part of a major refurbishment which opened up the courtyard to public access for the first time. Bronze memorial panels commemorating the fallen of the Second World War were relocated at the same time to frame the entrance from Leather Lane.

Part of the interior is now occupied by the headquarters of English Heritage.

Charterhouse

CHARTERHOUSE SQUARE, ECIM 6AN
LISTED: GRADE I

Closeted away behind high walls, and approached through a 15th century archway under an early 18th century house, the Charterhouse is a remarkable complex of mediaeval and later buildings. Little known to Londoners, it remains an introverted enclave of private almshouses for gentlemen pensioners.

In 1348-9 the site was bought by Sir Walter de Manny, who gave it to the City as a burial ground for victims of the Black Death, the cataclysmic pandemic which wiped out over half of Europe's population. In 1370 Manny founded a Carthusian monastery on the site, which became renowned as a refuge for spiritual retreat and contemplation. Between 1499 and 1503, Sir Thomas More prayed here wearing a hair shirt as a penance, but in 1535 it was ruthlessly suppressed by Thomas Cromwell following a dispute over the Oath of Supremacy. The Prior, John Houghton, was hanged at Tyburn, and then, while still alive, drawn and quartered. Subsequently it was occupied by Thomas Howard, the 4th Duke of Norfolk, who transformed it into a great ducal mansion from where he plotted against Elizabeth I, prompting his execution. In 1611 Norfolk's second son, Lord Suffolk, sold Howard House, as it was then known, to Thomas Sutton, "the richest commoner in England", for use as a school and almshouses. In 1870 the eponymous school moved away. Part was then redeveloped for Merchant Taylor's School, and later the Medical College of St Bartholomew's Hospital. Badly damaged in the Blitz, it still contains some magnificent historic interiors.

The Entrance Court leads to the Master's Court, which is faced in Kentish ragstone with mullioned windows under hood moulds. This incorporates the Great Hall, which lies off axis with the entrance gateway. Although much restored after the war by Seely & Paget, the interior is still an impressive historic space indicative of a late mediaeval hall in a private residence (opposite above right). The 16th century oriel window has carved spandrels and panelled jambs with the 16th and 17th century heraldic arms of Somerset and Sutton. The splendid screen (restored after the war) was installed by Norfolk in 1571 (opposite below). The gallery on the north wall with arcades and tapering pilasters was added by Sutton, as was the fireplace of 1614 designed by Edmund Kinsman. The original hammerbeam roof, burned in the war, was reinstated by Seely & Paget.

Adjoining the hall to the north is the Library with a range from the 1540s. A line of timber columns at ground level (p60 bottom right) supports the Great Chamber (left middle), above where both Elizabeth I and James I both once held court. Before war damage, it was regarded as the finest Elizabethan room in England, and it is still astonishingly atmospheric. Approached by a plain post-war oak staircase, it comprises a single large chamber with late 16th century decoration, including a fine timber and plaster chimneypiece with depictions of the Evangelists and Apostles, the Annunciation and the Last Supper carved into the columns and strapwork with a central panel repainted in 1626.

East of Master's Court, Chapel Court stands on the site of the original Carthusian chapel. Chapel Cloister (1613-4) (p60 top right) contains some fine early fragments including a 14th century tomb canopy and two 17th century figures of Moses and Aaron.

Beyond lies the present chapel (p60 top left), converted in the early 17th century from the early 14th century Chapter House. The north aisle of 1612-4 has Tuscan columns by Francis Carter, who was Chief Clerk of the King's Works under Inigo Jones. The upper stage of the tower and timber cupola were added in 1613. Within the chapel are some notable historic furnishings including a 17th century carved oak communion table, an organ gallery with tapering piers embellished with musical instruments and firearms, and a pulpit of 1613 with carving by Blunt. The excellent funerary monuments (p60 middle) include a recumbent Thomas Sutton (1615), a tablet and bust to John Law (1614) and another to Francis Beaumont (1624) alongside a legacy of 18th century memorials by Flaxman and Chantrey.

To the north of the Library, only half of the Norfolk Cloister (1571) survives including some entrances to monastic cells and the Priory Garden door.

Elsewhere, Washhouse Court is a highly evocative Tudor quadrangle of red-brick monastic outbuildings and lay brothers' accommodation inscribed with the initials of the unfortunate dismembered Prior Houghton. Pensioners Court to the north is from the 1830s by Blore. Preachers Court was reinstated following war damage with the Admiral Ashmore building, a well-considered new red-brick block by Michael Hopkins & Partners, completed in 2000.

Middlesex House of Detention

Clerkenwell Close, ec1r 0lt

Listed: Grade II

Concealed beneath the handsome brick and terracotta walls of the former Hugh Myddelton School in Clerkenwell Close lie the subterranean vaults of the old Middlesex House of Detention, a melancholic remnant of a much wider complex erected in 1846-7 to the designs of the county surveyor, William Moseley.

The House of Detention stood on the site of two earlier prisons – the Clerkenwell Bridewell, which closed in 1794 to be replaced by the nearby Coldbath Fields Prison at Mount Pleasant, and the New Prison, which was sacked in the Gordon Riots of 1780 and rebuilt in 1816.

By the 1840s the New Prison held 30 to 40 prisoners to a room, with lines on the floors to delineate areas for particular categories of inmate. To relieve this chronic overcrowding, a new short-stay prison was erected for those awaiting trial for petty crime. Conditions were strict, but not as fearsome as in the long-term correctional establishments. Although communication between prisoners was forbidden, they were allowed to wear their own clothes and to receive food and work materials from friends and relatives.

The new prison was modelled on Pentonville, which had been completed recently with long wings of cells radiating out from an octagonal central hall. Each cell had its own WC and basin and single small window. Ventilation and heating followed the same principle as Pentonville, with fresh air heated in the basement, circulated to the cells, then drawn off in flues and expelled by means of a central funnel over the octagon.

On 13 December 1867 the prison was the scene of the "the Clerkenwell Outrage" – the first Fenian bomb attack on London. A barrel of gunpowder was exploded beneath the exercise yard in a failed attempt to free Richard O'Sullivan Burke, an Irish arms dealer. The blast killed six bystanders and injured 50 others, damaging the houses in Corporation Lane (now Row) beyond repair. The incident triggered a huge backlash against the Irish cause amongst the British working classes. Karl Marx wrote: "One cannot expect the London proletariat to allow themselves to be blown up in honour of Fenian emissaries." The ringleader Michael Barrett was hanged outside Newgate Prison, the last person to be executed publicly in England.

After further enlargement, the surface buildings were levelled in 1890 for the Hugh Myddelton School, now converted to flats and offices. The basement of the cental octagon survives under the school, together with a grim range of vaults which once lay under the female wing, said to be haunted by the sound of a young girl sobbing, and which can be accessed from a narrow staircase and door off Clerkenwell Close.

During the Second World War the vaults were adapted and strengthened for use as an air-raid shelter. Wartime graffiti can still be seen on the walls.

Finsbury Town Hall

ROSEBERY AVENUE, EC1R 4RP

LISTED: GRADE II

With the reorganisation of London's civic government following the London Government Act 1899, the parishes of Clerkenwell, Charterhouse, Glasshouse Yard, St Luke's and St Sepulchre were all merged to form the new Metropolitan Borough of Finsbury.

The eclectic character of the town hall is as much a reflection of its phased development as its free Flemish Renaissance style. It was designed by Charles Evans-Vaughan, who won an architectural competition in 1893, and built in two stages. The first phase, completed in 1895, faced the newly formed Rosebery Avenue. The second, beneath an elaborate pediment carved with figures of Peace and Plenty, followed on five years later in a more florid Baroque style to replace an earlier parish watch house at the rear of the site, built in 1814 and enlarged in 1855.

Evans-Vaughan was commissioned to design the interior decoration. Whilst much of this is fairly conventional – glazed tiled dados and marble columns to the entrance halls and staircases – the Large Hall has a wide barrel-vaulted ceiling divided by plaster strapwork terminated by an apsidal west end decorated with plaster figures representing music and poetry. However the real highlights are the "Clerkenwell Angels". Sexy, draped winged female figures adorn the Ionic pillars bearing sprays of foliage with light-bulbs as flowers. The figures, modelled by Jackson & Co, and the elaborate brachiated light fittings, by Vaughan and Brown of Hatton Garden, impart a strong sensual Art Nouveau flavour to the entire hall, and are one of London's hidden delights.

The building is now the home of the Urdang Dance Academy.

Masonic Temple
Andaz Liverpool Street Hotel

40 Liverpool Street, ec2m 7qn
Listed: Grade II

Situated on the site of the first Bethlehem Hospital founded in 1247, the former Great Eastern Hotel was a late addition to the Liverpool Street Station complex and completed in two stages – the original range by Charles and Charles Edward Barry in 1880-4, and a later extension by Colonel R W Edis between 1898 and 1901. Originally the hotel had 160 bedrooms, but only 12 bathrooms. A set of dedicated railway tracks into the station regularly supplied provisions and salt water from Harwich for the hotel baths.

Externally it is a rather rambling, red-brick, gabled affair with mullioned and transomed windows in a vaguely French idiom, but internally some fine spaces can be found.

The dining room has an impressive central dome of coloured glass surrounded by elaborate plasterwork. During the Second World War it was swathed in mattresses and blankets to protect it from blast damage, which proved surprisingly effective. Only one small piece needed renewal, now marked in red glass. The former Abercorn Bar (now The George) resembles an Elizabethan coach house with a heavily embossed ceiling and dark oak panelled walls. A painting of Bishopsgate in the 17th century hangs over the bar. The former Hamilton Hall has rich plasterwork and painted scenes in rococo frames modelled on an apartment in the Palais Soubise in Paris. However, the real highlight of the interior lies hidden upstairs.

Up a fine marble staircase (by Edis) and through a maze of corridors is the mysterious Masonic Temple designed by Brown & Burrow in Greek style and completed in 1912 at a cost of £50,000 – equivalent to £4m today. A wood panelled antechamber leads through double doors into the Temple, which is set at a lower level and lined with 12 different varieties of Italian marble beneath a blue and gold ceiling decorated with the signs of the zodiac. At the centre is a gold sunburst with an illuminated central star. Around the perimeter is seating with two thrones set in mahogany aedicules adorned with Masonic symbolism. A bronze bust of the Duke of Connaught, the Grand Master, guards the entrance.

There is no truth in the assertion that the Temple was rediscovered by builders behind a false wall during the hotel's renovation in 1997. It is an urban myth, no doubt generated by the arcane nature of the room itself. A second temple in an Egyptian style in the basement by Edis was in poor condition and converted to a gym. Only the pilasters remain.

Drapers' Hall

THROGMORTON AVENUE, EC2N 2DQ

LISTED: GRADE II*

The Drapers' Company, which received its first royal charter in 1364, was the earliest corporate body in England to receive a grant of arms in 1439. Its first hall was in St Swithin's Lane, but in 1543 the company acquired its present site from Henry VIII, who had sequestered the original house and site from Thomas Cromwell following his execution. Successive buildings were ravaged in the Great Fire of 1666, and again in 1772, after which the rebuilt Hall was altered in 1868-70 by Herbert Williams, and again in 1898-9 by Sir Thomas Graham Jackson.

One might be forgiven for expecting the end result to be rather a dog's dinner, but nothing could be further from the truth. The interior is the finest Victorian livery hall with a grandiloquent suite of rooms which make Buckingham Palace seem homely. Indeed the Hall and Drawing Room have been used as alternatives to the Palace in various films, including *The King's Speech*.

Entered via a long oak panelled corridor lit by stained glass containing the arms of Drake, Nelson, Earl St Vincent and Raleigh, a grand marble and alabaster staircase in Quattrocento style rises to a spacious first floor landing under an elliptical ceiling. The walls are lined with Greek cipollino marble, the arcades of Ionic columns in Breccia marble and the doorcases in Emperor's Red marble. Between the Ionic columns are busts of Queen Victoria, Prince Albert and Frederick, Duke of York, together with Egyptian-style bronzes. Beyond is the Court Room, renovated by Herbert Williams in the 1860s but incorporating earlier 18th century work with magnificent Gobelin tapestries and portraits of Wellington and Nelson (opposite below left).

The Livery Hall (overleaf), enlarged by Williams, is a vision of breathtaking opulence. Marble Corinthian columns march around the entire room, paired in the apse, with each bay containing full-length royal portraits. The columns support a gallery and lunettes painted in a rather lurid purple hue. The vast ceiling, painted by the artist Herbert Draper, depicts scenes from *The Tempest* and *A Midsummer Night's Dream* with allegorical depictions of history, science, ethics and literature at each end. At the buffet end are two niches with 19th century statues of Hypatia by Richard Belt and Venus by John Gibson.

From the apse an oak panelled corridor leads to the plush Drawing Room (opposite above), designed by Herbert Williams and decorated by John G Crace in green and gold with a massive Victorian marble chimneypiece crowned by a segmental pediment and clock within a ram's head garland. On the wall is Herbert Draper's *The Gates of Dawn*, painted to mark the dawn of the 20th century.

Finally comes the Court Dining Room (opposite below right), a remnant of the 1667-71 reconstruction by Edward Jerman following the Great Fire, but comprehensively renovated in 1869 with a ceiling painting of *Jason and the Golden Fleece* by Barrias and a great coved cornice with the coats of arms of members of the Court. Two more Louis XV Gobelin tapestries depict the legend of the Golden Fleece.

Bank of England

THREADNEEDLE STREET, EC2R 8AH

LISTED: GRADE I

The Bank of England was born out of strategic necessity. In the late 17th century the need to rebuild a powerful navy dictated a revolution in national finances. A loan was raised and the subscribers were incorporated as the Governor and Company of the Bank of England with exclusive control of the government's balances, and the ability to issue banknotes. After its foundation in the Mercers' Company Hall, and a period at Grocers' Hall, in 1734 the Bank moved to Threadneedle Street where it expanded in stages with additions by Sir Robert Taylor in 1765-70, and then by Sir John Soane between 1788 and 1827, but by this time the distinctive blind screen walls, secure internal courts and top-lit banking halls were already established features.

During the First World War, the Court of Directors resolved to rebuild and expand the Bank within Soane's perimeter screen wall. Between 1923 and 1939 the Bank was reconstructed and extended upwards by Sir Herbert Baker. Plans to retain Taylor's and Soane's interiors proved impractical, although Baker's new top-lit perimeter banking halls closely follow Soane's original models. Taylor's Court Room and Committee Room were moved from the ground floor to the first, where they remain today.

Castigated by many for demolishing Soane's work and for reducing his noble perimeter wall to "a footstool for his work", for a long period Baker's reputation has been tarnished, the rebuilding condemned by Pevsner as "the worst individual loss suffered by London's architecture in the 20th century". In fact, Baker's work is a highly accomplished essay in the imperial classical style incorporating the very best materials and craftsmanship available.

Beyond a set of superb bronze doors by Charles Wheeler, the entrance vestibule has monolithic columns of black Belgian marble beneath a shallow vaulted stone dome. Below, on the floor, the central mosaic of St George slaying the dragon, taken from the reverse of the gold sovereign, is based on a design by Benedetto Pistrucci. Fine symbolic polychrome mosaics by Boris Anrep provide a continuous theme along the floors of the corridors. Beyond the vestibule is a double-height hall and gallery off which rises a magnificent open-well cantilever staircase leading to a colonnaded landing and the principal historic rooms. At the centre of the building the Garden Court was once the churchyard of St Christopher-le-Stocks, demolished for the Bank's expansion in 1782.

The Governor's Room and Ante Room contain fine paintings and furniture, the latter lined in red and gold damask with a Chinese Chippendale mirror (c1760) and oval desk (left and overleaf below middle). The lavishly carved alabaster chimneypiece of Apollo and the Muses (c1791) attributed to Sir Richard Westmacott is from Uxbridge House in Burlington Street, once the Bank's West End branch.

Taylor's relocated octagonal Committee Room is the economic nerve centre of the United Kingdom. It is in this room that the Bank's Monetary Policy Committee meets to set the Bank rate and national fiscal and monetary policy. The exquisite sage-green Court Room, terminated at each end by triple arcades, is the meeting place of the Court of Directors, full of allegory and symbolism: the winged head of Mercury representing trade, and over the Committee Room doors griffons guarding the mythical pile of gold at the earth's centre. The three marble chimneypieces are by Taylor, and the wind dial is a replica of the 1805 original which was used to forecast the arrival of shipping into the Pool of London and thereby anticipate its effect on commodity prices.

The Dining Room beyond, entirely by Baker, is in similar style and contains a fine set of glassware of 1855 by Daniel Maclise engraved with Britannia, the gift of the National Bank of Poland in 1946.

Midland Bank

27 Poultry, EC2

Listed: Grade I

Midland Bank was founded by Charles Geach in Birmingham in 1836. Over the next 20 years, by financing the expansion of its iron foundries, engineering companies and railways, it helped to transform the city into the workshop of the world. After a series of shrewd acquisitions, in 1891 it expanded its interests to London. By 1918, under its managing director and later chairman Sir Edward Holden, it had become the largest bank in the world, with deposits of over £335m and over 650 corresponding banks across the globe.

Holden was a firm believer in a corporate design policy. At the last general meeting before his death in 1919 he declared: "I have to report again that in modern days it is absolutely necessary to have good premises." Holden's successor as chairman was Reginald McKenna, the husband of Gertrude Jekyll's favourite niece, for whom Sir Edwin Lutyens had designed a house in Smith Square. In 1924 Lutyens was appointed to design the new bank headquarters in Poultry, working with Gotch and Saunders, who had designed many previous banks for the Midland. The vast pile which arose was one of the finest bank buildings in England.

Situated adjacent to the Bank of England and diagonally opposite the Royal Exchange, Lutyens produced a magnificent new building worthy of its wider setting and the pre-eminent status of the bank.

Externally it is Italian Mannerist in style, with giant austere elevations which rely for effect on subtle changes of surface modulation, including Lutyens' characteristic disappearing pilasters. Recessed behind the central aedicule is a shallow, saucer-shaped dome typical of Lutyens' work.

Internally it is gigantic. The double-height banking hall is divided into two intersecting axes by massive square Corinthian columns in green African verdite with white marble walls. The two axes meet at a circular marble light well (later converted to a reception desk) inset into the floor to light the safe deposit rooms below.

The lower level is reached by a giant Imperial staircase with a central niche and bronze statue of the *Boy with Goose* by Cecioni echoing the two on the front elevation by Sir William Reid Dick. There is a range of secure rooms with simple grilles for depositors to examine their safe deposit boxes in privacy. The safe deposit with its 25-ton door was built by the Chatwood Safe Company and displayed at the British Empire Exhibition in 1924. More recently it doubled as the setting for Fort Knox in the film *Goldfinger*.

High above at fifth floor level is the lush double-height Board Room surrounded by tapestries, the Directors' Dining Room and a superb range of oak panelled offices complete with purpose-designed furniture by Lutyens, including individual hat and umbrella cupboards for senior staff.

Currently vacant, the building is earmarked for conversion into a grandiloquent, seven-star hotel.

Lloyd's of London

1 LIME STREET, EC3M 7HA

LISTED: GRADE I

The Lloyd's building belies Oscar Wilde's famous dictum that nothing ages so fast as the truly modern. Thirty years after its completion in 1986, it remains as revolutionary and futuristic as when it first appeared. With its soaring vertiginous mass of pipes and services snaking up the outside of the building, its in-built flexibility and glistening, stainless steel carapace, it resembles some vast space age machine humming with the arcane world of high finance. Loved and loathed in equal measure when opened, it is now widely regarded as the ultimate exemplar of the High Tech style in Britain, and is one of only a handful of modern buildings to be listed Grade I.

Lloyd's takes its name from Edward Lloyd's coffee house, which began in Tower Street in 1686. It rapidly became the haunt of ship-owners and seafarers as well as the first underwriters who insured the ships and their cargoes. After moving to Pope's Head Alley in 1769, it relocated to the Royal Exchange in 1774 where it remained until 1928 when it moved to purpose-built offices designed by Sir Edwin Cooper with a vast new underwriters "Room" located behind a huge triumphal entrance arch.

Following an architectural competition, in 1978 the Richard Rogers Partnership secured the commission and produced one of the most innovative buildings of the late 20th century using the English members of the team that had overseen the Pompidou Centre in Paris.

Externally the concrete frame is articulated by six strongly-expressed service towers. Stainless steel round-ended staircase towers resembling giant ring binders soar upwards, while lines of replaceable stainless steel toilet cabins with porthole windows sit within their own concrete frame.

Inside, a huge, awe-inspiring central atrium rises 197ft skywards, culminating in a great barrel-vaulted glass roof executed with all the swagger and confidence of Joseph Paxton's Crystal Palace and the great mediaeval cathedrals.

On the ground floor is the Underwriting Room and famous Lutine Bell, traditionally rung once for the loss of a ship, and twice for her return. The first four levels of galleries are open to the atrium with banks of escalators rising through the centre, above which are enclosed floors reached via outside lifts, the first installed in the UK.

Bizarrely, for all its High Tech bravura, the ninth floor Board Room is a complete 18th century dining room by Robert Adam, which was removed from Bowood House in Wiltshire to an earlier 1950s Lloyd's building, and then reconstructed once again within the new building. The delicate plasterwork details and pastel colour scheme forms a surreal counterpoint to the High Tech building in which it sits, but it epitomises the City's ability to retain tradition alongside cutting-edge modernity.

Library and Geometrical Staircase
St Paul's Cathedral

EC4M 8AD

LISTED: GRADE I

Hidden from the public gaze in the south-west tower of St Paul's Cathedral is one of London's most awe-inspiring spaces – the Geometrical Staircase, which serves the Cathedral Library.

Andrea Palladio had illustrated various forms of spiral staircases in the first book of his *Quattro Libri*. Between 1629 and 1635 Inigo Jones introduced the first stone cantilevered staircase in England – the Tulip Stair – at the Queen's House in Greenwich, but for its colossal scale, structural ingenuity and sheer audacity Wren's Geometrical Staircase stands in a league of its own. It was built by the master mason William Kempster with delicate wrought-ironwork by Jean Tijou. Spiralling to the heavens, it swirls around the stone walls in two great revolutions up to the Cathedral Library, which is a veritable time capsule, virtually untouched since its completion over 300 hundred years ago.

The Library is contained in a huge stone chamber; the corresponding room on the north side of the cathedral, the Trophy Room, contains the famous Great Model of St Paul's. The chamber is lined with the original bookcases and dark oak panelling constructed under the watchful eye of Wren's master joiner, Sir Charles Hopson. Below the gallery, with its peculiar open balustrade, is an impressive sequence of timber console brackets intricately carved in 1709 by Jonathan Maine. Above, the stone mullions to the windows are also handsomely carved by Kempster with garlands of fruit and flowers playfully entwined around open books, inkwells and quills – an explicit reference to its function.

The Great Fire destroyed tens of thousands of volumes and much of the cathedral's original collections, but in 1713 Henry Compton, Bishop of London, bequeathed his collection to St Paul's, which accounts for his portrait hanging in pride of place over the original bolection – moulded marble chimneypiece. The Library has been added to ever since and now contains 16,000 books on theology. In 1710 Humfrey Warley, librarian to the Earl of Oxford, offered his collection of biblical editions to the cathedral, including one of only three priceless surviving copies of the first edition of Tyndale's New Testament, believed to have been printed in Worms in 1526. It is the Library's greatest treasure.

In 1710 the German bibliophile Zacharias Conrad von Uffenbach visited the Library and recorded what he saw: "The room is of moderate size, but very high, so that many books can be housed there. For in the upper part there is one shelf above another, which can be reached by a gallery … The Keeper of the Library is an Englishman, that is to say a person who concerns himself little about it … This place was somewhat dark for a library."

Today the librarian is both scholarly and diligent, but the room remains virtually exactly the same as when Uffenbach visited over 300 years ago: a place of great serenity haunted by the ethereal sound of the cathedral choir singing far below.

Central Criminal Court

OLD BAILEY, EC47EF

LISTED: GRADE II*

Inscribed over the entrance to the legendary Central Criminal Court are the words "Defend the Children of the Poor and Punish the Wrongdoer". Commonly known as the Old Bailey, the court is one of London's great landmark buildings, its distinctive dome modelled on the Royal Naval College, Greenwich. Crowning the dome, the gilt bronze sculpture of Lady Justice by F W Pomeroy has become a London icon – erroneously assumed to be blindfolded, and bearing the sword of punishment in her right hand and the scales of justice in her left. In the segmental pediment over the entrance are allegorical figures of Truth, Fortitude and the Recording Angel, also by Pomeroy.

The court originated as the sessions house of the Lord Mayor and Sheriffs of the City of London and Middlesex and was rebuilt several times. By the 19th century, the Old Bailey was a small courtyard adjacent to Newgate Prison, which was demolished amid great controversy to make way for a magnificent new building, the outcome of a limited architectural competition won by E W Mountford.

Erected between 1900 and 1907, it is a superb Edwardian Baroque composition, but because of restricted public access, its interior is relatively little known.

Behind the original entrance is a huge tripartite hall with double-aisled spaces framing an Imperial staircase in cream, green and white marble. The Grand Hall on the first floor with its huge domed centrepiece echoes St Paul's, with carved pendentives of the Virtues by Pomeroy. Friezes inscribed with elevating references run around the space, including "The law of the wise is a fountain of life" and "London shall have all its ancient rights". Severely damaged by a bomb in 1941, the paintings in the lunettes are post-war replacements by Gerald Moira depicting the emergency services, as are the rather lacklustre painted figures in the main dome and spandrels. The four original courtrooms open off this space. Around the halls are statues of Charles I, Charles II and Sir Thomas Gresham taken from the tower of the second Royal Exchange, as well as a series of eminent Victorian and Edwardian figures including the prison reformer Elizabeth Fry by Alfred Drury (1913).

Some of the most famous trials in British legal history have taken place at the Old Bailey. Dr Crippen, Lord Haw-Haw, the Kray Twins, Ruth Ellis, Dennis Nilsen and the Yorkshire Ripper were all called to account here.

Adjacent is a contextual extension by Donald McMorran and George Whitby completed in 1972, beneath which is a short section of Roman city wall and an even earlier cemetery which contained some fine funerary ware. A year after the completion of the extension, the Provisional IRA exploded a car bomb in the street outside. A glass shard remains embedded in the wall at the top of the stairs as a reminder of the incident.

Ye Olde Cheshire Cheese

WINE OFFICE COURT, 145 FLEET STREET, EC4A 2BU
LISTED: GRADE II

Unlike so many London pubs, which have been ruined by unthinking modernisation, Ye Olde Cheshire Cheese enjoys layer upon layer of history which confer a timeless sense of antiquity. William Sawyer, a late 19th century regular, wrote of it: "No new-fangled notions, no new usages, new customs, or new customers for us. We have our history, our traditions and our observances, all sacred and inviolable."

Built in 1667, directly after the Great Fire, the rambling, labyrinthine interior offers a rare glimpse of the atmosphere of a late 18th century chop house and tavern. Marked by an old circular 19th century lantern, the entrance, off Wine Office Court, is through a late 18th century shopfront. To the right of the door is a list of the 15 monarchs who have reigned during the pub's lifetime. Another celebrates its distinguished visitors, which reads like a roll-call of the giants of English literature: "Here came Johnson's friends, Reynolds, Gibbon, Garrick, Dr Burney, Boswell and others of his circle. In the 19th century came Carlyle, Macaulay, Tennyson, Dickens, Forster, Hood, Thackeray, Cruikshank, Leech and Wilkie Collins. More recently came Mark Twain, Theodore Roosevelt, Conan Doyle, Beerbohm, Chesterton, Dawson, le Gallienne, Symons, Yeats and a host of others ... "

The interior is wonderfully evocative. On entering, to the right is the Gentlemen's Bar, a dark-stained early 18th century room with an open fire, next to which Charles Dickens used to sit beneath a full-length 1829 portrait of William Simpson, a former waiter, which was commissioned by the clientele of the time as a measure of the esteem in which the old retainer was held. Dickens was a frequent visitor, and in *A Tale of Two Cities* it is the model for the pub to which Sydney Carton takes Charles Darnay after his acquittal for treason.

To the left is the Chop Room with booths of high-backed oak settles; its once-renowned 80lb meat puddings stuffed with beef, kidneys, oysters, larks, mushrooms and spices being mentioned in Galsworthy's *Forsyte Saga*. Here are Dr Johnson's chair and *Dictionary*. Although there is no documentary evidence Johnson ever visited, it is highly unlikely he did not, as the pub adjoins one of the approaches to his house beyond in Gough Square. In 1923 the eminent Soviet writer Boris Pilnyak visited and wrote a story in Russian *Staryi syr* or *Old Cheese*, which is set in the pub.

A fine late 18th century staircase leads to a series of panelled upper floor rooms which are used for private dining. Downstairs in the basements is a warren of vaulted cellars which predate the pub and are believed to originate from an earlier 13th century Carmelite monastery which stood on the site.

For many years the Cheese was the home of Polly, a foul-mouthed parrot, now forever mute, who sits stuffed perched serenely in the ground floor bar (opposite centre). On Armistice Night 1918 she imitated the popping of champagne corks over 400 times before keeling over and fainting. Polly's death in 1926, aged 40, was announced to a distraught public on BBC Radio and in over 200 newspaper obituaries around the world.

Daily Express Building

120-129 FLEET STREET, EC4A 2BE

LISTED: GRADE II*

The former *Daily Express* building (now Goldman Sachs) was the first curtain-walled building in London; a revolutionary exercise in uncompromising modernism described at its opening in 1932 as "Britain's most modern building for Britain's most modern newspaper".

Commissioned by its Canadian proprietor, Lord Beaverbrook, the architect was Sir Owen Williams (1890-1969), who took over the work from Ellis and Clarke, who had proposed a more conventional, masonry structure. Williams was originally an aircraft designer and engineer by training, who made his name with a series of bold concrete buildings for the British Empire Exhibition at Wembley in 1924, including the famous Empire Pool, and later the iconic Boots factory in Nottingham. His final work in the late 1950s was the design of the M1 motorway.

By providing a concrete basement box, Williams doubled the unobstructed width of the printing hall and clad the entire structure in sleek black Vitrolite with streamlined chromium-stripped horizontal fenestration, its glowing ribbons of light symbolising a newspaper that never sleeps.

The result was described anthropomorphically by the influential modernist Serge Chermayeff as "frankly elegant in tight-fitting dress of good cut which tells with frankness and without prudery the well-made figure wearing it".

In complete contrast to the smooth functional exterior, the entrance foyer is a complete riot – a full-blooded Art Deco romp inspired by Hollywood and the architecture of the American cinema. It was designed by Robert Atkinson (1863-1952) and is, quite simply, one of the finest surviving examples of its style in Britain.

At the centre, hanging over the entire hall, is a huge Expressionist-style pendant lantern surrounded by zig-zag, back-lit coving set in a silver and gilt starburst ceiling. The walls are lined with travertine above a rosewood dado with a black marble plinth and stainless-steel fittings. The floor is inlaid with serpentine patterns resembling waves of the sea. Beyond is a wonderful sinuous spiral staircase.

As if this was not enough, the highlight of the hall are the fantastic plaster reliefs designed by Eric Aumonier (1899-1974) representing industry. At each end are large relief panels in silver and gilt. One depicts Britain as the great workshop of the world, complete with a steam locomotive and liner. Opposite is *Empire* – a superb evocation of the people, flora and fauna from a community of nations on which the sun never set – complete with stylised elephants, writhing snakes, ostriches and kangaroos.

In 1961 the interior featured in the science fiction film *The Day the Earth Caught Fire*.

Rudolf Steiner House

35 PARK ROAD, NW1 6XT

LISTED: GRADE II

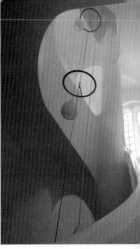

B orn in Croatia in 1861, Rudolf Steiner – philosopher, architect, mystic and social theorist – was the founder of anthroposophy, a new spiritual movement which attempted to fuse science and mysticism by exploring a union of the rational and the numinous. In later life his ideology was expressed increasingly through art and architecture and "eurythmy", a new art form based on the expression of movement. The little-known London centre, Rudolf Steiner House, is arguably the most important expressionist building in Britain.

For a period in his late 20s, Steiner edited the Goethe archives in Weimar and was influenced strongly by his philosophy. "Just as the eye perceives colour and the ear sounds, so thinking perceives ideas." As leader of the German-Austrian branch of the Theosophical Society, Steiner refined his esoteric and spiritual interests before breaking away in 1912 to form a new group, the Anthroposophical Society. Based at Dornach in Switzerland, Steiner established The Goetheanum, an extraordinary cultural centre built of concrete in an organic expressionist style which was completed in 1928, three years after his death.

A year before he died, Steiner gave his blessing to a new building in London on a site in Park Road, close to Regent's Park. Designed by Montague Wheeler (1874-1937), a pupil of E P Warren, it was built in stages between 1924 and 1938 in cast concrete with granolithic facings. Externally the only hints of expressionist design are in the curved eyebrow hood mould over the shopfront and in the stylised entrance doors, but internally it is remarkable, with sinuous organic staircases reminiscent of the work of Steiner's contemporary Antoni Gaudí in Barcelona, and Erich Mendelsohn's Einstein Tower in Potsdam.

Commenting on his own work, Wheeler wrote: "No forms have been employed for the sake of tradition, and the materials used have been shaped in the manner in which their nature seems to suggest." In his "free and plastic use of concrete", originally modelled in clay, Wheeler closely followed Steiner's principles, to release "its real potentialities". The staircases, restored in 2008, are washed in water-based pastel pigments which enhance the impression of movement and light, and confer an ethereal, spiritual quality on the whole interior.

The main hall, with its expressionistic curves and angles and decoration by Baron Arild Rosenkrantz, was designed as a stage for performances of eurythmy, a profound philosophical concept which permeates the form and design of the entire building, including the serpentine patterns on the terrazzo floor, which were revealed as part of a major restoration in 2007-8.

In his advocacy of ethical individualism, Steiner was a prophetic holistic thinker and polymath who anticipated many current issues, including biodynamic agriculture (the precursor of organic farming), complementary medicine, developmental work for those with disabilities, racial tolerance and educational freedom from government control.

Of the 17 buildings designed by Steiner, three have been cited as being amongst the most significant works of modern architecture, yet he remains relatively unknown.

The Black Friar

Built near the site of a Dominican friary established in 1279, which subsequently conferred the name Blackfriars on the entire area, the eponymous Black Friar now stands isolated on a wedge-shaped site at the junction of Queen Victoria Street and New Bridge Street.

The original pub was a fairly conventional affair, built in 1875, but in 1905 the interior was remodelled in high Arts and Crafts style for a publican by the name of Petit by H Fuller Clark with the sculptors Henry Poole and Frederick Callcott to create a riotous mediaeval fantasy of "Merrie England". Poole was master of the Art Workers Guild. Here craftsmanship was deployed in the service of fun and as a secular parody of the rich ecclesiastical interiors of the time. Jolly fat friars cavort and carouse in a range of worldly pursuits interspersed with life-enhancing homilies.

The lush interior is clad in pink, green and cream marble with ornamental friezes and panels of jovial friars in copper, bronze, timber and mosaic. Over the fireplace with its corner seats is a bas-relief of singing friars entitled *Carols*. A stained-glass window shows a friar in a sunlit garden. Above the bar another frieze – *Tomorrow will be Friday* – shows monks catching trout and eels.

Beyond is the Grotto, built in 1917 by Clark as an extension into the adjacent railway arch, over which is another frieze – *Saturday Afternoon* – portraying monks gardening, enriched with lustrous coloured enamels.

Beneath the mosaic vaults and mirrors of the Grotto are mottoes of wisdom – "Finery is Folly" and "Don't advertise, tell a gossip" – the latter with monks doing their weekly washing. Elsewhere, *A Good Thing is Soon Snatched Up*, is a vignette of a pig trussed up in a wheelbarrow, while beneath the cornice are devilish imps representing music, drama, painting and literature. Quotes from Aesop's *Fables* and nursery rhymes were executed in elaborate gilt lettering by the Birmingham Guild, while the lamps hang from fittings of carved wooden monks carrying yokes on their shoulders.

Today it seems inconceivable that such a magnificent testament to British craftsmanship and creative imagination should have been threatened, but in the 1960s demolition was seriously mooted and only averted following a public campaign led by Sir John Betjeman. It is yet another example of a superb historic building only saved through the efforts of a handful of enlightened individuals who were prepared to challenge established orthodoxy.

Sion College

56 Victoria Embankment, EC4Y ODZ

Listed: Grade II

Sion College, situated close to Blackfriars Bridge, was established in 1624 under the will of Thomas White, the vicar of St Dunstan's in the West, as a college, guild of parochial clergy and almshouses at a site on London Wall. It was soon augmented with a library donated by Dr John Simson, one of White's executors. Ten years after receiving its royal charter in 1630, it had become a stronghold of London Presbyterianism.

After various vicissitudes, including extensive damage in the Great Fire, in the 1850s the college expanded its membership and took on the examination of boys in the City's Ward and National Schools, triggering its relocation to a new site on the Victoria Embankment at Blackfriars Bridge.

The new building was designed in a Perpendicular Collegiate Gothic style by Sir Arthur Blomfield, the son of the Bishop of London from 1828 to 1856 and a former Fellow and Visitor of the College. It was opened by the Prince and Princess of Wales on 15 December 1886. The most innovative feature of the new complex was a large two-storey porch and forecourt which were carried over the District Line beneath on an elliptical brick arch. Unfortunately the porch was demolished in 1965 for the Blackfriars Underpass, and replaced by a low, slit-windowed extension by Ronald Ward & Partners.

Internally, the galleried and clerestoried library sits beneath a deal hammerbeam roof. The great south window overlooking the Thames has post-war stained glass of historical figures designed by Cox & Barnard in 1951. In 1944 the City Livery Club co-located and shared the premises, but in 1996 the college was dissolved and its collections relocated to Lambeth Palace Library and the Maughan Library, King's College, London. It is now in use as private offices.

Blizard Institute of Cell and Molecular Science

4 Newark Street, e1 2at
Unlisted

The Blizard Institute is named after the surgeon Sir William Blizard, who founded the London Hospital Medical College in 1785. Blizard was described by John Abernethy, who later established the St Bartholomew Medical School, as "the beau ideal of the medical character", who would say: "Let your search after truth be eager and constant … Should you perceive truths to be important make them the motives of action, let them serve as springs to your conduct". Abernethy commented: "I cannot readily tell you how splendid and brilliant he made it appear, and then he cautioned us never to tarnish its lustre by any disingenuous conduct, by anything that wore even the semblance of dishonour."

These qualities are as relevant today, as the quest for scientific truth lies at the heart of the Blizard Institute. However, there is nothing remotely traditional about the eponymous building with its sleek lines of curtain walling incorporating coloured glass artwork by Bruce McLean. The architect, Will Alsop, one of Britain's most original and idiosyncratic architects, allowed his creative imagination full rein, symbolically treating the inside of the building as an organism. His characteristic trademark pods occur in wildly different forms housing seminar rooms and meeting spaces within the atrium. The Cloud Pod resembles a large eyeball, while a large orange cluster – the Centre of the Cell – is a public exhibition space entered via a bridge with views into the laboratories beyond. The 400-seat lecture theatre has light fittings resembling illuminated platelets.

Intended to open up medical research and engage the public in the process, the £45m building is one of London's most striking new architectural landmarks, housing a world-class centre for interdisciplinary collaborative medical research.

Wilton's Music Hall

GRACE'S ALLEY, E1 8JB
LISTED: GRADE II*

Wilton's Music Hall is the oldest of its kind in the world – the only remaining example of a first-generation grand music hall. It is hauntingly atmospheric, with a pervading aura of romantic decay, which presents a real conservation challenge. It requires a very light touch if the fabric and distressed finishes are to be saved, and its existing fragile, character preserved.

Like many buildings of its kind, its history is accretive. Its nucleus was the "small, and not very respectably conducted" Prince of Denmark public house, believed to be the first in London to boast mahogany bars and fittings – hence its nickname the Old Mahogany Bar. The first concert room – the Albion Saloon – existed behind the pub, licensed in 1843 to a Matthew Eltham.

In 1850 John Wilton, the manager of the well-known Canterbury Arms music hall in Lambeth, acquired the building, and, according to contemporary accounts, "rid the house of the irreclaimable. Quiet has superseded riot, and order disorder." Soon after he bought the neighbouring properties, behind which he constructed a much larger hall to the designs of Jacob Maggs. After various changes of ownership, and a disastrous fire in 1877, it was rebuilt by J Buckley Wilson of Wilson, Wilcox and Wilson of Swansea with a raked floor and proscenium arch, reopening briefly as Frederick's Palace of Varieties. However, its new incarnation was short-lived. In 1888 it became a mission hall, and later a rag-sorting depot and warehouse before it was acquired in 1963 in an enlightened intervention by the Greater London Council. It is now owned by Wilton's Music Hall Trust.

The entrance hall is simply the enclosed paved yard of the original tavern. A narrow staircase leads to a warren of small supper rooms tainted with the aura of scandalous liaisons. Given its proximity to the docks, prostitution was rife and music halls were notorious for soliciting. Traces of the original painted plasterwork remain. Ad hoc development hid a multitude of gimcrack structural solutions, including the use of salvaged railway tracks as girders to support the floors.

The main hall is one of London's hidden wonders – a long, thin apsidal-ended auditorium with an elliptical barrel-vaulted ceiling. Around three sides is a gallery carried on barley-sugar columns with the balcony fronts decorated with carton pierre, or papier maché, decoration by White & Parlby. The faded plaster walls have paired recesses which once held a glittering array of mirrors. At one end the high stage is framed by a proscenium arch, whilst in the centre of the auditorium space for supper tables was surrounded by promenades for standing customers. Other than some charred ceiling joists, alas nothing now remains of the colossal sunburner chandelier once brilliantly illuminated by over 300 gas jets and 27,000 crystals. The burner, built by Defries & Son, was renowned as "a solid mass of richly-cut glass in prismatic feathers, spangles and spires".

Wilton's attracted the usual mixture of the entertaining, the exotic and the bizarre. Particular highlights included M Rotae, the Hungarian contortionist, the Brothers Ridley, celebrated acrobats, and Herr Whautkins, a flamboyant Anglo-German who "wound up his feats of dexterity by juggling with flaming torches". One critic avidly awaited "a dissolving diorama of the Ascent of Mt Blanc" which was to be added to the programme that week. George Leybourne, the original Champagne Charlie, performed here, and it is alleged that Wilton's was the scene of the first London display of the can-can after which it was immediately banned.

Wilton's is of immense social, historical and cultural significance. Every effort should be made to preserve it for future generations.

St George's German Lutheran Church

ALIE STREET, E1 8EB

LISTED: GRADE II*

Tucked away in the backstreets of Whitechapel, St George's is the oldest surviving German Lutheran church in Britain, with a beautifully preserved 18th century interior, now the headquarters of the Historic Chapels Trust which was responsible for its salvation.

The church was founded in 1763 to provide a place of worship for the émigré German merchants who dominated the sugar industry of east London, having brought their expertise to the capital from the Baltic Hanseatic towns in the mid-16th century. At its height there were around 16,000 German Lutherans in Whitechapel alone. Its principal benefactor was Dederich Beckman (c1702-66), a wealthy sugar refiner, who donated the huge sum of £650 towards the total of £1,802 needed to build the church. Beckman is believed to be buried beneath the communion table. His son-in-law, Gustavus Anthony Wachsel, was the first pastor. Shortly after his appointment, Wachsel was responsible for assisting over 600 Germans who were abandoned in London in 1763 en route to St John and St Croix. Wachsel's appeal raised over £600. The Tower of London gave 200 tents for temporary shelter, and the King intervened directly to enable them to travel instead to Carolina.

The architect was probably Joel Johnson, a local carpenter turned architect who worked with Boulton Mainwaring on the nearby London Hospital and who was responsible for St John's, Wapping. The modest pedimented exterior has a central Venetian window flanked by two doorcases. The original bell tower was demolished in 1934.

The delightful and little-changed interior is filled with rare original grained and numbered box pews surrounded on three sides by timber galleries carried on eight timber Doric columns also with box pews set in raked rows. At the liturgical east end is a high pulpit approached by a short set of stairs with a tester above carrying a gilded dove. Flanking the pulpit are two large commandment boards with German inscriptions in Baroque style carved with scrollwork and cherub heads, probably by Errick Kneller in 1763. Above are the gilded royal arms of King George III. At the opposite end, the organ is by the Walcker family using the earlier organ case. The stained-glass window of the Crucifixion is an early work of Powell & Sons, part of a refurbishment carried out in 1855.

A door at the foot of the vestry staircase leads to a small courtyard that until 1855 was the chapel's cemetery, which was later enclosed by a German Infants' School by E A Gruning, now converted to flats. Wachsel's successor as pastor, C E A Schwabe, was also chaplain to Queen Victoria's mother, the Duchess of Kent, who was patron of the school and a regular worshipper.

In 1930 Dr Julius Rieger was appointed pastor. Rieger was an associate of Dietrich Bonhoeffer (1906-45), a theologian and vehement opponent of National Socialism, who served as a pastor elsewhere in London in 1933-5 and preached in the chapel in 1935. The church became a relief centre, providing advice and shelter for German and Jewish refugees in the pre-war period. Bonhoeffer was hanged at Flossenberg concentration camp in April 1945, days before the war ended.

The church was taken into care by the Historic Chapels Trust in 1999, and restored in 2003-4 at a cost of £900,000. Wachsel's collection of over 750 rare books was handed to the British Library for safe keeping.

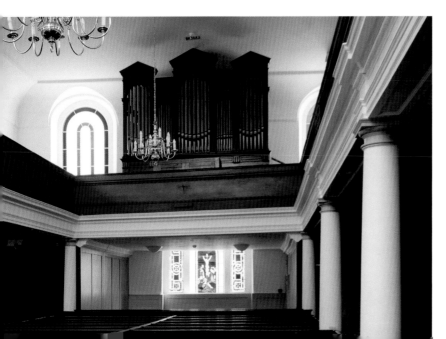

18 Folgate Street

E1 6BX

LISTED: GRADE II

There is nothing remotely like 18 Folgate Street anywhere else in London. Its dream-like, fantasy interior was the life's work and vision of Dennis Severs (1948-99), an oddball but gifted American collector, who acquired the house as a shell in 1979. Over the next 20 years he painstakingly assembled each room as a sequence of experiences or "spells" reflecting the decoration, furnishings, textures, light, sounds and even smells of different periods of the past from 1724 to 1914. Meticulously researched, many of the finishes were mocked up in the manner of stage scenery using inexpensive materials like discarded timber from the nearby Spitalfields Market to replicate panelling or chimneypieces. All is artifice. Nothing is what it seems, yet it conveys a haunting sense of the past embalmed.

Marked by a bracketed Windsor lantern over the entrance door, externally there is little to distinguish the three-bay-wide house of 1724 from its neighbours, other than the unusual trellis pattern carved into the box frames of the first floor sash windows. However, on entering, the visitor is transported into an atmospheric time warp as though walking through a frame into a painting with a time and life of its own, where he becomes part of a *tableau vivant*, part theatre, part fantasy, part invisible performance art and part still-life drama. The visitor experiences each room in silence, absorbing the moods and ambience of each as a mute witness. Severs's aim was to give visitors "a rare moment in which they become as lost in another time as they appear to be in their own".

Severs invented an entirely fictional silk-weaving family – the Jervises – around which the experiences revolve. Half-eaten food and half-filled wine glasses lie strewn around the rooms amongst bowls of fruit, guttered candles and pungent pomanders as if the family has just left the room as one enters. Recorded sounds of the 18th century city outside and from next-door rooms are used to startling theatrical effect to convey the impression of being a silent observer of everyday household life. Clocks chime. A canary chirps. The stairs creak and whispers can be heard just outside the door.

The smoking room is artfully arranged to reflect the Hogarth picture which hangs within it: the miasma of cigars pervading the air. The drawing room is aggrandised and dressed with garlands of walnut shells (opposite below). The boudoir above is left as though the occupants have just risen, with an unmade bed and unemptied chamber pot. As one rises through the house to the top floor the scene shifts to Dickens's London and abject poverty. Washing is hung across the staircase; the paint is peeling. Cobwebs hang in the corners. A thick layer of dust coats every surface and rags hang at the windows.

For all its artifice, stagecraft and illusion, 18 Folgate Street conveys a much more compelling presentation of past London life than the rather sterile, sanitised approach of the great heritage organisations and museums. The motto of the house is "Aut Visum Aut Non!" – "You either see it or you don't". Totally bonkers and utterly wonderful.

Paget Memorial Mission Hall

18-26 Randells Road, n1 0dh

Listed: Grade II

Hidden behind an unprepossessing terrace of late 19th century houses, the Paget Memorial Mission Hall is a poignant tribute to a wife from her grieving husband, and one of London's most bizarre ecclesiastical buildings.

Violet Mary Paget, the daughter of Lord Alfred Paget, was a Mildmay deaconess, who held Bible classes in a temporary iron hut on this site in 1887-9, prior to her marriage to the Reverend Sholto Douglas, later Lord Blythswood. On her death in 1908, her distraught husband was touched to receive a letter of sympathy from one of her pupils and resolved to acquire the site and build a permanent mission hall in her memory. Designed by Beresford Pite, it was opened in the presence of a large number of relatives and friends by HRH the Duchess of Albany on 20 May 1911.

The hall was one of many undenominational missions founded to offer spiritual guidance and social welfare to the deserving poor, but the Paget was unique because it incorporated a wealth of much older 17th and 18th century artefacts, taken from the music room at Sholto Douglas's home at Douglas Support in Lanarkshire following a disastrous fire. While much of the interior can be attributed to Pite, the whole extraordinary melange is quite unlike any other mission in the country.

The pulpit is embellished with two late 17th century Venetian walnut torchères with figures depicting Vice and Virtue beneath a broad oak pediment carrying the arms of Lord Blythswood and memorial panels to his wife's Bible class. Over the lunette window above, and beneath a fine Jacobethan roof, are uplifting evangelical inscriptions, including "The Word of the Lord Endureth For Ever."

Around the perimeter the arcaded panelling is divided by carved cartouches carrying the monogram "VP" by Martin Travers, a pupil of Pite. Running along the cornice above are stencilled gilt violets – a recurrent decorative motif also found carved in the pulpit rails.

A great organ loft bears the organ from Douglas Support carved on four barley-sugar columns with bulbous bases. Adjacent is a simple, pedimented chimneypiece with an overmantel portrait of Violet, but on the south wall are two grotesque chimneypieces, one with a lion rampant in low relief crowned by three statuary figures, the central one of Christ after Thorwaldsen. The other incorporates original Jacobean carving with two massive twisted columns on huge carved bases.

In the Leader's Room is the original Minton breakfast set, a gift to the couple from Queen Victoria.

W Martyn

135 Muswell Hill Broadway, N10 3RS
Listed: Grade II

Martyn's is the best-preserved traditional grocer's shop in London. It is virtually unchanged since it was established by the owner's great-grandfather, William Martyn, in 1897. William was born in 1862 in Broad Clyst, Devon, and moved to London in 1890 where he was an apprentice at the Hampstead branch of Walton Hassell and Port before opening his own business seven years later in the new suburb of Muswell Hill, a highly successful piece of town planning laid out by James Edmundson and W J Collins between 1896 and 1914. Martyn's is the only surviving original occupier of the first range of shops to be opened in Queens Parade at the heart of the new suburb.

Externally, the shop was altered twice in the inter-war period, but it retains black Vitrolite stallrisers and a fascia bearing the name W Martyn in white raised block capital letters.

Inside is a wonderfully atmospheric grocer's shop from the early 20th century, with produce displayed in the traditional manner. The shop has simple matchboarded linings to the walls with twisted barley-sugar columns and fluted pilasters to the display shelves. Running along one side is a panelled mahogany counter, behind which are semi-circular storage bins with hinged wooden lids and lines of drawers. In front of the counter are old metal biscuit barrels, stacked goods and sacks of coffee. At the rear the hatch to the original cash desk remains.

The shop is currently run by third and fourth generation members of the Martyn family.

Georgian Orthodox Cathedral Church of the Nativity of Our Lord

ROOKWOOD ROAD, N16 6SS

LISTED: GRADE II*

What is now the Georgian Orthodox Cathedral was once the Ark of the Covenant, the spiritual home of the Agapemonites, one of the more colourful Christian sects that emerged in the 19th century.

Known as the Community of the Son of Man, the Agapemonites emerged in the 1840s as followers of Henry Prince, a renegade Anglican minister who established a religious commune – the Agapemone, or Abode of Love – at Spaxton in Somerset. His followers sold their possessions, which funded the development of the commune, and, in 1892-5, an extraordinary church in Clapton for non-resident believers.

The church is a striking composition with a tall Gothic tower, needle spire and four corner turrets each bearing the inscription "God is Love". Four huge apocalyptic bronze winged figures by A G Walker of a lion, an ox, an eagle and an angel taken from the Book of Revelation stand silhouetted against the sky. These are repeated in stone below, trampling underfoot tiny winged human figures representing the trials of earthly life – death, sorrow, crying and pain.

Inside, a great hammerbeam roof covers the entire space. Around the apse is a mosaic band with representations of *The Pelican in her Piety* and *The Phoenix* alongside an inscription from John 11:25: "I am the Resurrection and the Life". The nave benches, fittings and Willis organ are all original, although a later altar has replaced the original throne on which the minister sat. The glory of the interior is the spectacular, semi-opaque stained glass designed by Walter Crane and executed by J S Sparrow depicting Old Testament imagery, symbolic flora and allegorical scenes in a variety of Art Nouveau and Arts and Crafts patterns. The west windows, inspired by the illustrations of William Blake, show a central sun rising over the sea of life with aquatic creatures flanked by windows depicting disease and death and sin and shame with writhing figures tortured by flames and snakes. The whole jolly ensemble encapsulates the eccentric apocalyptic beliefs of the Agapemonites.

In the 1860s Henry Prince achieved notoriety by proclaiming himself the incarnation of the Holy Spirit and practising free love with his harem of attractive women acolytes, but this was nothing compared to the controversy caused by his successor, John Smyth-Pigott, a tall, emaciated figure with glittering black eyes, who on 7 September 1902 suddenly announced from his throne to an astonished congregation: "I who speak to you tonight, I am that Lord Jesus Christ who died and rose again and ascended to heaven. I am that Lord Jesus come again in my own body to save those who come to me from death and judgement."

Smyth-Pigott's blasphemous antics generated "one of the most disgraceful scenes that have ever desecrated an English Sabbath". A full-blown riot ensued, to which police reinforcements were called. Shortly afterwards Smyth-Pigott retreated to the Agapemone, where the "Dear Beloved" consoled himself with his numerous "spiritual brides".

The building later became the Church of the Good Shepherd used by an arm of the Ancient Catholic Church. After lying vacant for several years, it was acquired recently by the Georgian Orthodox Church, which has done excellent work repairing and restoring one of London's more bizarre ecclesiastical buildings.

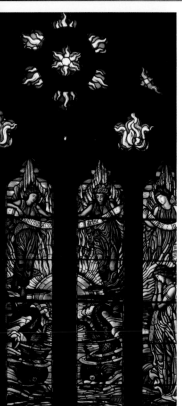

L Manze

76 High Street, e17 7ld
Listed: Grade II

E el, pie and mash shops are unique to London and those nearby seaside towns which are frequented by East End families such as Southend. They were started by a small number of families, the Cookes, the Manzes and the Burroughs, all of whom subsequently intermarried.

The Manze family was among the second wave of Italian immigrants who arrived in Britain in the late 19th century and who grew to specialise in popular catering. Michele Manze arrived from Ravello in southern Italy at the age of three in 1878. The family settled in Bermondsey, making a living as ice merchants, and later ice-cream makers. Recognising the need for cheap, nutritious meals catering for the working classes, Michele Manze set up a chain of eel, pie and mash shops. The first shop, established at 87 Tower Bridge Road in 1902, still survives. Thirty years later there were 14 bearing the Manze name, including this one in Walthamstow.

The interior is a superb survival of an early 20th century working-class restaurant. The terrazzo floors are strewn with sawdust. At the entrance is a long marble-topped counter complete with the original cash register. The walls are lined throughout in white ceramic tiles with a dark green and white tiled chequerwork dado divided by rectangular brown edge-tiled panels containing bevelled-edge mirrors. A tiled frieze of green and brown garlands runs in a continuous ribbon around the top of the walls. Below, the tables are set in bays between the original mahogany benches with acorn finials lit by two lines of pendant light fittings above.

Woolwich Town Hall

WELLINGTON STREET, SE18 6PW

LISTED: GRADE II

W oolwich is believed to take its name from the Anglo-Saxon for "trading place for wool", although there is evidence of earlier Roman and Iron Age settlements. For centuries it was synonymous with England's military-industrial complex, a connection which continues to this day. The Royal Arsenal had already been in place for 40 years when Henry VIII founded the Royal Dockyard in 1512. Given its strategic location on the river commanding the route into London, it soon developed into a garrison town. The Royal Military Academy arrived in 1741, followed by the Royal Artillery Barracks (1776-1802), whose colossal attenuated Georgian façade is the largest continuous elevation in the country.

With the reorganisation of local government, in 1900 Woolwich was amalgamated with Eltham and Plumstead to form the new Metropolitan Borough of Woolwich. A magnificent new town hall was erected which boasts one of the finest civic interiors in London.

Designed between 1903 and 1906 by (Sir) Alfred Brumwell Thomas, the architect of Belfast City Hall, it is a florid essay in the Baroque Revival executed with real panache. The soaring red-brick and stone clock tower is a prominent local landmark, but the real *tour de force* is the interior, which is a self-confident expression of Edwardian civic pride in one of London's poorest neighbourhoods. It was opened on 13 January 1906 by the local Labour MP, Will Crooks.

Victoria Hall, the voluminous, triple-domed and galleried hall, is truly imperial in scale, with a staircase dominated by a fine white marble statue of Queen Victoria by Frederick W Pomeroy embellished with rich ornamental plasterwork, coffered arches and elaborate pendant lights. Stained-glass windows by Geoffrey Webb depict notable local historical events, including the visit of Charles I to the dockyard in 1637 to see his great ship the *Sovereign of the Seas*. The elegant domed council chamber retains its original finely carved joinery.

Crossness Engine House

BELVEDERE ROAD, SE2 9AQ

LISTED: GRADE I

Crossness Sewage Works is a crucial component of the most important public infrastructure project ever built in London. Hailed as a masterpiece of Victorian engineering, the engine house is a veritable cathedral of ironwork.

In the 50 years from 1800, London's population rose from 1.1 million to 2.7 million without any commensurate investment in the sanitary infrastructure required to support such a growth. The concept of environmental health was as alien to most Victorian minds as the connection between dirt and disease. Cholera was believed to be spread by a miasmatic vapour. Urban life was a nightmare for the poor. Cholera, typhoid, the white plague (TB) and typhus stalked the capital. Over 10,000 Londoners died in the cholera epidemic of 1853-4. Four years later, during the long hot summer of 1858, the Great Stink overshadowed the city: a smell so pungent that plans were made to evacuate the House of Commons.

As a result of public outrage, the Metropolitan Board of Works, which had been founded two years earlier, was empowered to construct a vast new sewerage system for the metropolis under the enlightened direction of its chief engineer, Sir Joseph Bazalgette (1819-91).

Bazalgette devised a visionary engineering solution. Three massive intercepting sewers were built running parallel to the river. Hidden beneath great embankments, these were ovoid in shape to optimise flow and facilitate self-cleaning, diverting foul water from the old sewers and culverted rivers eastwards to great holding tanks at Abbey Mills and Crossness, where it was pumped into the river on the ebbing tide.

Opened in April 1865 by the Prince of Wales, and designed by Bazalgette and the architect Charles Henry Driver, Crossness is a wonderful expression of the exuberance and confidence of the Victorian age. Behind the plain grey gault and red brick exterior, the spectacular engine house is a riot of Victorian ironwork containing four beam engines built by James Watt & Co, named Prince Consort, Victoria, Albert and Alexandra. With 52-ton flywheels and 47-ton beams, they are believed to be the largest rotative beam engines in the world.

In 2003 Prince Consort was restored to working order by the Crossness Engines Trust, which has managed the site since 1987 and is restoring the entire complex to its former glory with the benefit of grant aid from English Heritage and the Heritage Lottery Fund.

A memorial bronze of Bazalgette can be found in central London at the foot of Northumberland Avenue on the Embankment, which he created.

Danson House

DANSON PARK, BEXLEYHEATH, DA6 8HL

LISTED: GRADE I

Once London's most notorious and intractable building at risk, Danson House was saved from dereliction by the direct intervention of English Heritage, which acquired the house in 1995.

Danson is the epitome of the perfect Palladian villa – so chastely detailed and impeccably proportioned that one might be forgiven for thinking it was on the outskirts of Vicenza rather than the more prosaic suburbs of Bexleyheath.

It was designed by Sir Robert Taylor and built between 1764 and 1767 for Sir John Boyd, a West Indian sugar merchant from St Kitts, later deputy chairman of the East India Company. Raised on a hill above the surrounding landscape, it remains a prominent landmark. A 1782 guidebook commented: "The house presents itself to the view of every traveller, between ten and eleven milestones on the Dover Road". Standing in over 600 acres, the estate was landscaped by Nathaniel Richmond in 1761-3 including sweeping lawns and a lake, beyond which was an eyecatcher in the form of a "Gothick" cottage with a thin tapering lead spire, which still survives in Blackfen Road.

After the death of Sir John in 1800, his son demolished the original wings and built a detached stable block to designs attributed to George Dance the Younger, but seven years later the estate was sold to John Johnson, a retired army captain. In turn, in 1863 his son sold the estate to a local railway engineer and developer, Alfred Bean, in whose family it remained until the death of his widow in 1924, at which time it was acquired by Bexley Urban District Council as a public amenity. During the Second World War the house was given over to civil defence duties, after which it went into progressive decline. In February 1991 it reached its nadir when a lessee stripped the interior of its chimneypieces, doorcases, doors and plasterwork. Fortunately the chimneypieces were retrieved by HM Customs, and the remaining artefacts were found a year later in a container in Dagenham.

Between 1996 and 2005 English Heritage carried out an award-winning restoration of the house in three distinct phases, culminating in the restoration of the interiors aided by a set of 1860 watercolours by Sarah Johnson.

At the centre of the house is a magnificent elliptical cantilevered stone staircase rising to an elliptical dome carried on eight Ionic columns surrounded by painted *trompe-l'oeil* stone coffers. The entrance hall has been restored to its original colour scheme, while the octagonal Saloon has been reinstated with real panache with replicated mirrors, based on the Johnson watercolours, and blue chinoiserie wallpaper. In the library the rare surviving domestic chamber organ built by George England has been lovingly restored.

Reopened by the Queen in July 2005, responsibility for the house has been transferred to the Bexley Heritage Trust.

Danson House is a triumph. It demonstrates that even the most dilapidated historic buildings can be saved from ruin through determination and vision, and that expert historical and technical research is essential in striking the right balance between careful conservation and informed restoration.

Rivoli Ballroom

346-350 Brockley Road, se4 2by

Listed: Grade II

The Rivoli Ballroom is a rare surviving example of a full-blown 1950s conversion of a former cinema to a dance hall catering for the age of jazz, swing and rock and roll.

Designed by Henley Attwater, it opened as the Picture Palace cinema in 1913 opposite Crofton Park Station in the suburbs of Lewisham. After various changes of venue, it was refurbished, extended and reopened in 1931 as the Rivoli Cinema seating 700. For the next 26 years it remained independently operated, until 1957 when it closed in the face of competition from the big cinema chains and television. After two and a half years lying dormant, it was adapted and converted to a ballroom by Leonard Tomlin, a local businessman and enthusiastic dancer, whose relative had been a lessee of the original cinema in 1917.

The plush interior is a creative amalgamation of Art Deco, neo-classical and Oriental motifs to create an exotic venue for the increasingly affluent teenagers of the 1960s. The raked foyer, lined with Deco-style parquetry panels in dark wood inlay with diamond-shaped glazed centres, leads to the spectacular ballroom – a long barrel-vaulted room with a raised viewing dais, proscenium and stage with fixed banquette seating and a purpose-built, sprung Canadian maple dance floor. The lush exuberant décor of red velour padded walls, gilt panels, scallop lights, French chandeliers and Chinese lanterns is wonderfully kitsch and redolent of the period of winkle-pickers and flared skirts.

Along each side are two long narrow bars – one lined with booths and tables in leather upholstery resembling a railway carriage, the other with a front of tiled, interlaced Arabesque patterns. Beyond is a separate late 20th century function room with a ceiling covered in prints of Old Masters.

Now achingly fashionable, many will recognise the offbeat interior as a backdrop for music and fashion shoots, DVDs and television series. There is nothing quite like it anywhere else in London.

Crosby Hall

DANVERS STREET, SW3 5AZ

LISTED: GRADE II*

History likes patterns. In one of those peculiar chronological resonances that echo through the history of London, a mediaeval City merchant's house is being restored to its full splendour, over 500 years after it was first built, by a modern City financier to form the centrepiece of a phenomenal new riverside home for himself and his family. Quietly but inexorably, a vast new private palace has arisen beside the Thames in Chelsea to provide the perfect setting for Crosby Hall, London's most important surviving domestic mediaeval building. It is the fulfilment of a vision which has inspired its benefactor, Christopher Moran, for his entire adult life.

Crosby Hall was built in Bishopsgate between 1466 and 1475 for Sir John Crosby, a wealthy City merchant, diplomat and ardent Yorkist. It was later occupied by Richard III, as Duke of Gloucester, and Sir Thomas More, after which it enjoyed a chequered existence as an early headquarters of the East India Company, a Dissenters' chapel, a warehouse and latterly a restaurant. Threatened with demolition, it could have been destined for the roof of Selfridge's, but in 1910 it was dismantled and relocated to Chelsea by the LCC under the watchful eye of the architect Walter Godfrey, where it was re-erected on the site of part of Sir Thomas More's old garden for subsequent use by the British Federation of University Women. In 1988 it was acquired by Moran, who embarked on one of the most remarkable post-war building projects London has seen.

Advised by a team of eminent experts, a great neo-Tudor mansion has been crafted painstakingly over the past 15 years as an authentic setting for the original hall and Moran's own spectacular collection of 15th and 16th century furniture and paintings. It is a glorious celebration of British craftsmanship and the full-blown reimagining of a stately Tudor mansion constructed over a period of 150 years, but one accurately modelled on a variety of historical precedents.

The entrance range, inspired by Hampton Court, leads to an Elizabethan garden designed by the Marchioness of Salisbury with an ornamental fountain of Diana by Neil Simmons derived from one at Nonsuch Palace. Beyond, Walter Godfrey's old building has been completely reworked and embellished to form the Council Chamber (p120 bottom and p121), which is approached through a grand Corinthian doorcase. The massive oak door (opposite below left) is embellished with the head of Medusa and inlaid on its inner face with intricate marquetry work.

The room beyond is breathtaking. Over the fireplace is a huge bronze of the owner embellished with his personal motifs – the sea stag and stars. To one side a traditional spyhole hidden in the plasterwork enables the host to time his entrance before his guests to maximum effect. At one end of the chamber is an oak staircase with carved sea stag newel posts leading to a gallery and on into the original great hall; at the other, to an antechamber (the Star Chamber) and on into the huge dining room (below), modelled on Kirby Hall in Northamptonshire, the centrepiece of which is a massive oak dining table hewn from a single 45ft length of timber and lit by heraldic stained glass in the fashion of the late 16th century.

On the upper floors a new long gallery is coming to fruition (right), but it will be several years yet before the whole remarkable vision is fulfilled, including a full-blown chapel beneath the original great hall where, fittingly, the owner will lie for eternity in his private mausoleum in a building which is a monument to his single-minded vision.

Battersea Power Station

CRINGLE STREET, SW8 4NB

LISTED: GRADE II*

With its sublime external silhouette that has made it one of London's most iconic riverside landmarks, Battersea Power Station is also its most conspicuous listed building at risk, and the largest brick building in Europe.

It was built over a period of 25 years by the London Power Company as two individual power stations side by side. Station A was begun in March 1929, but not completed until 1935, was only complemented by its identical twin, Station B, in 1953-5 when the fourth, south-east chimney was completed. In its heyday the site provided one-fifth of London's entire electricity supply; the most thermally efficient power station in the world had 338ft-high chimneys fitted with water and alkaline scrubbers to minimise sulphur emissions and atmospheric pollution. The waste heat was used to power the Pimlico district heating scheme.

Both stations were designed to form a coherent whole under a design team led by S Leonard Pearce with Henry Allot as consulting engineer, but in order to appease public opinion, exercised at the construction of such a monumental industrial complex on the banks of the Thames, Sir Giles Gilbert Scott was brought in to remodel the exterior with his characteristic use of sparse but subtle ornamental brick detail of brown Blockley brick cladding over a colossal steel frame.

The inside of Control Room A overlooking the original turbine hall, is like a vision from Fritz Lang's *Metropolis*. It is the work of J Theo Halliday in an extraordinary transmutation of Art Deco cinema design to an industrial utility. The quality of the finishes is astonishing. The walls are lined with Ribbon Napoleon marble, with black Belgian marble fluting to the windows. The ceiling is divided into eight huge bays, each coffered and glazed with linear decorative lighting and the original Halophane light fittings. The original L-shaped control panel and walnut veneer furniture all still survive in front of an intriguing array of levers and dials.

The post-war Control Room B (right middle), which opens directly into its own turbine hall, is plainer, but nonetheless impressive, with faience cladding and an arc of stainless steel control panels. Above, the upper control room, added in the 1950s, retains its banks of control desks and panels.

The power station remains one of London's most intractable conservation problems. Since its closure in 1983, it has defeated three major attempts by developers to adapt and convert the building as part of a massive regeneration of the wider area. Its long-term future remains uncertain, but behind its forlorn brick shell lies one of London's most atmospheric and awe-inspiring spaces.

Chapel of St Francis of Assisi
HMP Wormwood Scrubs

W12 0AE

LISTED: GRADE II*

Approached through a portal resembling some great mediaeval gateway, the gatehouse to HMP Wormwood Scrubs is one of London's most unusual architectural and cultural icons. On each of the flanking octagonal towers, terracotta roundels depicting the great prison reformers Elizabeth Fry and John Howard look down in reproach and compassion on those entering below.

The inmates certainly needed the latter, as the prison was designed by Sir Edmund Du Cane, a belligerent former military engineer, who became chairman of the Prison Commission following the 1877 Prison Act. Du Cane was a strict disciplinarian who saw it as "his fate to take up the harsh penal regime ... and by effective administration realise its full punitive potential".

To reduce costs the prison was built entirely by convict labour between 1874 and 1891 and to an innovative plan, which departed from the Pentonville model of radiating wings in favour of a "telegraph pole layout" with four parallel cell blocks linked at their centre by covered walkways. This was derived from the pavilion hospitals which had been promoted by Florence Nightingale following her experiences in the Crimean War. Wide blocks orientated from north to south were intended to promote the circulation of fresh air and to ensure that each cell received some sunlight during the day. Communal ablution blocks were introduced as individual toilets and basins in each cell fostered foul air and disease. The model was influential and other examples were built at Bristol, Norwich, Shrewsbury and Nottingham.

The Victorian penal system placed great emphasis on silent contemplation and Bible reading. As a result the chapel at Wormwood Scrubs is the largest and finest prison chapel in England, capable of accommodating 1,000 inmates. Designed by Du Cane in French Romanesque style, the wide nave and narrow aisles ensure maximum security and visibility. Huge arch-braced tie-beams in dark stained oak carry kingposts which support the diagonally boarded roof. A rhythm of seven bay arcades of moulded round arches on thick drum piers surrounds the nave, terminated by an apsidal-ended sanctuary with round-arched panels of saints. The lunette above depicts scenes from the life of Christ, all allegedly painted by prisoners, who were led through the east and west doors via covered walkways from the adjacent cell blocks.

Notable alumni include the spy George Blake, who escaped on 22 October 1966, Oscar Wilde's lover Lord Alfred Douglas, the Labour minister John Stonehouse, who faked his own death, and the rock musicians Keith Richards and Pete Doherty.

Stockwell Bus Garage

BINFIELD ROAD, SW4 6ST

LISTED: GRADE II*

Given the shortage of steel for major infrastructure projects in post-war Britain, necessity was the mother of invention. A number of highly innovative buildings were erected with futuristic roof structures that were a combination of architectural bravura and cutting-edge engineering.

London Transport had a long tradition of pioneering progressive new architecture and design. In 1937 Oliver Hill designed a bold new bus station for Newbury Park comprising seven semi-circular concrete arches with open ends. As a result of the Second World War it was eventually built 10 years later, and it encouraged a vogue for similar structures.

At the time of its construction in 1952 Stockwell Bus Garage was the largest area under a single roof in Europe. The architects Adie, Button & Partners and the engineer A E Beer used post-war shortages to their advantage and produced an heroic feat of engineering for a utilitarian public purpose.

Formed from ten shallow, double-hinged ribs graduating in depth from 10ft 6in at the ends to 7ft in the centre, the soaring, whale-backed roof spans 159ft across 73,350 square feet of unobstructed floorspace capable of accommodating 200 double-decker buses. Between each pair of ribs, cantilevered barrel vaults filled with a network of glazed rooflights permit bands of light to stream down, flooding the interior. Externally the flowing roofline is supported on angled buttresses enclosed by repetitive bays of vertical lights and double doors.

Stockwell was highly praised at the time. It fostered other innovative roof structures, including the famous hyperbolic paraboloid roof over the Commonwealth Institute in 1962 (by Robert Matthew, Johnson-Marshall & Partners), and the lesser-known shallow elliptical paraboloid dome over the rebuilt Poultry Market at Smithfield (1963 by T P Bennett & Sons), to which it passed the accolade for the largest clear span in Europe.

Gala Bingo Club

50 MITCHAM ROAD, SW17 9NA

LISTED: GRADE I

Better known in its former incarnation as the Granada Cinema, the Gala Bingo Club is the only Grade I listed cinema in England, and one of the most lavish to be found anywhere in Europe.

It opened on 7 September 1931 as the flagship of Sydney Bernstein's Granada empire, featuring Jack Buchanan and Jeanette McDonald in *Monte Carlo*. The architect of the exterior was Cecil Masey (1881-1960), who produced a fairly conventional and rather restrained landmark in an Italianate style covered in white faience with a towering central entrance articulated by four tall Corinthian columns in antis. But in an age of architectural fantasy what set the Granada apart was the astonishing interior, designed by the colourful theatre designer and impresario Theodore Komisarjevsky.

Komisarjevsky (1882-1954) was a director in the Imperial and State Theatres in Moscow. After the Russian Revolution he moved to England in 1919, where he won acclaim as a set designer and modernist producer at the Shakespeare Memorial Theatre, Stratford upon Avon, culminating in a brief marriage to Dame Peggy Ashcroft.

Within is pure fantasy. Five sets of double doors lead into a lobby in quasi-mediaeval style, beyond which is a huge foyer in the form of a baronial hall. At the far end are twin flights of Travertine stairs leading to the balcony. In the void between the rake of the balcony and its soffit is the extraordinary Hall of Mirrors (below) beneath a barrel-vaulted ceiling encrusted with plaster flowers and lined with long arcades of cusped arches inset with pier glasses.

But the real climax lies beyond: the colossal auditorium, designed to seat 3,000, has an intricate coffered Gothic ceiling, arcaded walls and gabled Gothic canopies suspended over the proscenium arch. To each side are huge Gothic gables decorated with painted murals of troubadours and mediaeval figures including a wimpled maiden and a Negro drummer boy, all executed by the artists Lucien le Blanc and Alex Johnstone.

Under the stage, now converted to a café, is a full-blown 14-rank Wurlitzer organ, which was originally installed in a theatre in Sacramento, California, together with a four manual organ console in the old orchestra pit. The organ was restored in 2007, but damaged by flooding shortly after.

The Granada was equipped for stage shows and variety artists as well as film, and in the 1950s and 60s was the venue for many leading artists of the day including Danny Kaye, Frank Sinatra, the Andrews Sisters, Frankie Laine and Jerry Lee Lewis, but with declining audiences it closed as a cinema on 10 November 1973 with a final showing of *The Good, the Bad and the Ugly*. It remained unused until it reopened as the Gala Bingo Club on 14 October 1976.

Leighton House

12 Holland Park Road, w14 8lz

Listed: Grade 1

Leighton House, the studio-home of the eminent Victorian artist Frederick, Lord Leighton (1830-96), boasts one of the most exotic interiors in London. Triumphantly restored in 2010 by the Royal Borough of Kensington & Chelsea, its jewel-like Arab Hall radiates once more with all the gorgeous extravagance of the East: a romantic vision of the Orient distorted through very Victorian eyes.

The house was built in stages over 30 years, in close collaboration between Leighton and his architect, George Aitchison, the Professor of Architecture at the Royal Academy and president of the RIBA from 1896 to 1899.

Leighton had very definite ideas of the house he wanted. In 1864 he wrote to his father that "architecture and much ornament are not inseparable", but the first phase of the house was a restrained classical affair in red Suffolk brick and Caen stone with little hint of what was to follow. It comprised a north-facing studio and gallery, and, in the interests of propriety, a separate side entrance for his models.

In 1879 a major extension was completed to the west of the house for Leighton's extensive collection of Islamic tiles which he had acquired during various trips to the Near East. Modelled on the palace of Zisa in Palermo, the magnificent Arab Hall is coruscated with hand-painted ceramics from the 14th, 16th and 17th centuries punctuated by Damascene latticework screens. The centrepiece is a fountain and pool set in a floor of elaborate Victorian mosaic surrounded by ottoman seats. But the lustrous Arab Hall was not some self-indulgent exercise in the reuse of architectural antiquities; it was designed for maximum dramatic aesthetic impact and incorporated the work of some of the leading artists of the time. The capitals to the smaller columns are by Sir Joseph Edgar Boehm, the gilded birds on the carved caps of the large columns are the work of Randolph Caldecott, whilst the wonderful gilt mosaic frieze was made in Venice by Walter Crane. The iridescent cobalt-blue tiles to the staircase and corridor are by William de Morgan.

As a gentleman, orientalist, collector and artist, Leighton saw it as part of his mission to educate the masses, so during his trips abroad, the London poor were allowed to trudge through the house in a noble attempt to elevate their aesthetic sensibilities.

In 1889 Aitchison built a winter studio to the east of the house, and in 1927 the architect Halsey Ricardo was commissioned to design the Perrin Galleries which lie beneath it.

On Leighton's death in 1896, attempts were made to offer the house and its contents to the nation, but sadly much of the collection and furniture was sold and dispersed. In 1925 it was acquired by Kensington Borough Council. As part of the recent restoration many of the original paintings have been loaned back, and, after painstaking research, the furniture and furnishings have been spectacularly reproduced to match the originals.

The Thematic House

LANSDOWNE WALK, W11 3LN
UNLISTED

Few architectural theorists have the practical skills necessary to translate their intellectual concepts into reality, but at the Thematic House Charles Jencks – architect, landscape designer, theorist and polymath – has done just that. Between 1978 and 1983, with the aid of Terry Farrell, Piers Gough, Michael Graves and other architect friends, the promoter of post-modernism remodelled his conventional 1840s London town house into a remarkable statement of his own world view: that architecture should directly address the question of meaning through the rediscovery of symbolism and metaphor.

The Thematic House is imbued with 22 different levels of meaning around the themes of cosmic time (the seasons and passage of the sun and moon) and cultural time (the rise and fall of civilisations). Everything within the house from the front door to the Cosmic Loo has a deeper meaning and resonance, but all shot through with irreverence, wit and humour.

Windows and doors are abstractions of the human body. The front door leads to the Cosmic Oval with a mural by William Stok depicting the Big Bang (above right) and the creation of the universe, beneath which are portraits of some of the world's great free-thinkers – from Imhotep and Pythagoras via Erasmus and John Donne to Borromini and Thomas Jefferson.

The ground floor rooms are organised around the spiral Solar Stair, an abstract representation of the solar year with 52 steps for the weeks of the year, 7 divisions for the days of the week, 365 grooves, and stainless-steel spheres to the handrails symbolising the sun, earth and moon. Beneath is a spiral mosaic by Eduardo Paolozzi of a black hole which echoes the spiral of the handrail.

Each of the ground floor rooms is dedicated to the cycle of seasons. Winter has a bust of Hephaestus modelled on the features of Paolozzi, and Spring busts of April, May and June sculpted by Jencks's sister are raised on pedestals. Beyond, the Sundial Arcade has a huge remotely-controlled window overlooking the garden. The centrepiece of Summer is a brilliantly-inventive expandable table inspired by the sun. The kitchen on the theme of Indian Summer is littered with visual puns and witty references including "spoonglyphs" – triglyphs made of wooden spoons celebrating the pleasure of food alongside Hindu deities. Autumn is decorated in burnt red with Egyptian ankh symbols of femininity decorating the cupboards.

Upstairs is Jencks's library and office and other thematic rooms including the Four Square Room reminiscent of Mackintosh. Light is drawn down to the landing and dressing rooms by the Moonwell – a shaft of mirrored surfaces designed by Ilinca Cantacuzino.

Jencks stands in the long tradition of single-minded architects from Pugin to Lutyens whose work was underpinned by an underlying intellectual rigour and deeper layers of meaning. Inexpensive materials and artifice have been deployed with imagination and humour to create a total architectural experience which eloquently demonstrates that modernity should not be confused with modernism.

Warrington Hotel

93 WARRINGTON CRESCENT, W9 1EH

LISTED: GRADE II

Guarded by a small detachment of K2 telephone kiosks, the Warrington Hotel occupies a prominent corner of the Church Commissioners' Maida Vale estate from which a series of avenues radiates outwards from a central rond-point. Built in 1859 as an hotel, the sedate stucco façades conceal a riotous interior which borders on the promiscuous, adding weight to salacious allegations that the hotel was once a brothel.

Beneath a huge shell niche, mosaic steps flanked by tiled Corinthian columns and octagonal iron lamps lead to the plush interior, which is a theatrical revelation. Stained-glass windows and etched and cut-glass screens divide the bars, the walls lined with arcades of bevelled-edged mirrors separated by twisted mahogany columns. The centrepiece is a sweeping semi-circular marble-topped bar with mahogany panels divided by console brackets. Behind is a magnificent array of bar fittings – glass screens, mirrors and scrolled brackets – culminating in a sinuous overhead canopy decorated with cavorting cherubs.

In 1965 the canopy and walls were painted with some wonderfully erotic Pop Art Nouveau nudes by Colin Beswick, calculated to inflame the thirst of even the most abstemious. So well executed that many believe them to be original, they are an eloquent demonstration that period interiors can be enhanced by high-quality contextual alterations carried out in the original style.

At the rear of the saloon a huge semi-circular niche with Art Nouveau stained glass and lamps, and yet more erotic nudes, add to the louche atmosphere. To one side, beyond a screen of marble pillars, is a grey marble chimneypiece with neo-Jacobean strapwork. The lower flight of the massive staircase has a thick serpentine handrail leading to the upper floors over which sits a stained-glass lantern.

Once the watering hole of jockeys, one of whom is alleged to have won a £100 bet by riding a horse into the bar, the current clientele seem to prefer the more refined pleasures of the first floor restaurant.

Harrow School

HIGH STREET, HARROW, HA1 3HP

LISTED: GRADE I AND II*

Harrow School was founded by a local yeoman farmer, John Lyon, under a royal charter of Elizabeth I in 1572. On his death 20 years later, Lyon left money for the maintenance of the road to London and for a new school building, which was completed in 1615. Widely regarded today as one of the best schools in the world, before 1845 Harrow had a harsh reputation. Anthony Trollope recalled bitterly, "I was never spared, and was not even allowed to run to and fro between our house and the school without daily purgatory". Later, as a teenager, he was an outcast: "I had not only no friends, but was despised by all my companions." By the late 17th century the custom of boarding boys in houses dispersed around the neighbourhood was established, a practice which continues to this day.

Under the headship of Dr Charles Vaughan, a pupil of the reformer Thomas Arnold at Rugby, between 1845 and 1859 the school was transformed, and the numbers expanded to accommodate demand.

The Old Schools lie to the west of the High Street in a characteristic Tudor building with crowstepped gables and oriel windows. But appearances are deceptive. Externally Lyon's original building, designed by Sly, was enlarged and refaced by C R Cockerell in 1819-21, but the interior retains an astounding 17th century schoolroom, the Fourth Form Room, which is lined with fielded panelling covered with the names of generations of past pupils as incised graffiti, including Byron and Sheridan. At the north end is a simple hooded throne for the headmaster. Opposite is an usher's chair. The long sides of the room are lined with forms, or benches, for the boys, interrupted only by a large stone fireplace of 1730. Above lies the Governor's Room with panelling from 1661-2.

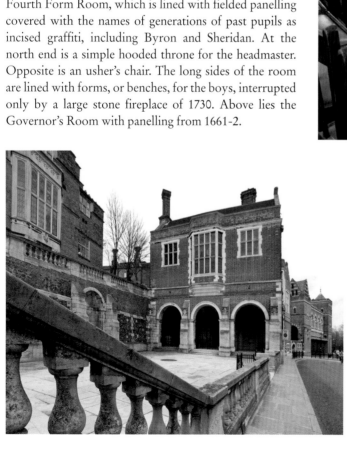

The Speech Room of 1874-7 was a tercentenary project designed by William Burges – a huge, idiosyncratic D-shaped space on a classical plan, but with rampant Gothic detailing which Burges planned to embellish with Moorish decoration *à la* Cardiff Castle, but unfortunately he died before its completion. The stained glass is by J C Bell.

The War Memorial building (1921-6, by Sir Herbert Baker) created a formal approach to the Old Schools and reconfigured the area with broad steps and terraces added in 1929. The War Memorial is an austere domed and vaulted crypt with a simple stone catafalque to mark the sons of Harrow that fell in the First World War. Inside is a vaulted hall and stone stair enriched with timber and bronze panels inscribed with a poignantly long roll-call of names of those who fell across the Empire between the First and Second World Wars. The hall and staircase contain a fine range of busts including Peel by Noble (1850), Palmerston by Johnson (1870), and Churchill by Clare Sheridan (1941).

The architectural climax of Baker's building is totally unexpected – the Alexander Fitch Room (opposite below) is lined with superb Elizabethan fittings from Brooke House, Hackney, complete with a stone fireplace, fluted pilasters and a huge plank table in pride of place at the centre of the room.

Amongst the many alumni are seven British prime ministers including, most notably, Winston Churchill, as well as Sir Robert Peel, Lord Palmerston and Stanley Baldwin. Other distinguished former pupils include Admiral Rodney, Jawaharlal Nehru, Lord Shaftesbury, Field Marshal Alexander and not least Lieutenant Teignmouth Melville, who died trying to save the colours after the disaster at Isandhlwana during the Zulu War, one of 19 Old Harrovians who have received the Victoria Cross.

Shri Swaminarayan Mandir

105-119 Brentfield Road, NW10 8LD
Unlisted

The scientist Charles Steinmetz wrote: "Some day people will learn that material things do not bring happiness." This is why one of the more surreal pleasures of a trip to IKEA in Neasden is the glorious sight of the Shri Swaminarayan Mandir rising serenely above the dreary townscape of the mutilated suburban houses that line the North Circular Road.

The Mandir was the first traditional Hindu temple to be built in Europe, and the largest outside India. Completed in 1995, it is one of the seven wonders of modern Britain and a magnificent testament to Indian craftsmanship: 2,828 tons of Bulgarian limestone and 2,000 tons of Carrara marble were despatched to India, where a team of over 1,500 sculptors and masons carved the stone for over two years. The 26,300 components were then shipped back and reassembled in London in a sort of giant 3D jigsaw puzzle. Funds were raised entirely by the Hindu community, including children collecting and recycling aluminium cans. It was opened in August 1995 by the spiritual guru and head of the organisation Pujya Pramukh Swami Maharaj, who has written:

"A mandir is a centre for realising God.

A mandir is where the mind becomes Still.

A mandir is a place of paramount Peace.

A mandir inspires a higher way of Life.

A mandir teaches us to respect one another."

Designed by the architect C B Sompura, the £12m Mandir is the focal point of a wider complex including a *haveli* – a multi-functional cultural centre – and an ashram for resident *sadhus* (monks). Raised high on a stone platform, seven tiered shikharas crowned by golden spires adorn the serrated roofline, complemented by five ribbed domes.

Within is a series of seven shrines housing sacred *murtis* (depictions of Hindu deities) which are attended each day by *sadhus*. Each surface is carved profusely with sacred figurative sculpture expressing spiritual symbolism through posture, hand gestures and facial expressions. Sinuous ribbons of beautifully carved stone link the arches to convey a sense of weightlessness and levitation.

The adjacent *haveli* of English oak and Burmese teak (opposite below left) is carved with stylised animal heads, flowers, garlands and iconography in a cornucopia of patterns taken from the traditional courtyard houses of Gujarat. Within lies a vast prayer hall unobstructed by intermediate columns which can accommodate 3,000 people.

The Mandir is a rich and exotic addition to London's architectural heritage and the living embodiment of Britain's special relationship with India.

No 11 Group Operations Room

RAF Uxbridge, ub10 orn

Listed: Grade I

In the summer of 1940, hour upon hour, day after day, the fate of Britain and the entire free world was determined by the tactical decisions taken in this bunker. It was from here that a handful of RAF pilots turned the tide of history in the skies over London in one of the epic battles of the 20th century, inflicting a decisive strategic defeat on the Luftwaffe which altered the whole direction of the Second World War.

In 1939 Britain had the most sophisticated layered air-defence system in the world. Three years earlier a new strategic headquarters had been created for Fighter Command at RAF Bentley Priory (p432), with four group sector stations around the country. No 11 Group Operations Room at RAF Uxbridge was responsible for the air defence of London and south-east England.

Construction of the bunker began in August 1937 and was completed ten days before the outbreak of the Second World War. Located 60ft underground, it was designed to withstand a direct hit from a 500lb bomb.

During the Battle of Britain overall control was exercised from Bentley Priory by Air Chief Marshal Sir Hugh Dowding. From there information on air threats was received from the Royal Observer Corps and radar stations around the country, sifted, assessed and passed to the four group operations centres to co-ordinate action from individual sector airfields.

On 16 August 1940 Churchill visited the bunker to watch the battle in progress. He was profoundly moved. As he left with tears streaming down his face he remarked to General Ismay: "Never in the field of human conflict has so much been owed by so many to so few," a phrase which he used four days later in his legendary speech to the House of Commons. King George VI and Queen Elizabeth visited on 6 September. Churchill returned again at the climax of the battle on 15 September – now Battle of Britain Day – as the last remaining RAF squadrons were sent into battle. "How many reserves have we?" Churchill asked, to which Air Vice Marshal Keith Park replied, "There are none."

Later in the war, General de Gaulle, Lord Mountbatten and Anthony Eden all visited. Air support for the Dieppe Raid in August 1942 and for the Normandy Landings on 6 June 1944 was co-ordinated from here.

In 1975 the bunker was refurbished by 9 Signals Unit. The map table was restored and the sector signal boards returned to their appearance on 15 September 1940. Today it is a museum which can be visited by groups by prior arrangement.

The events controlled from this unprepossessing bunker on the outskirts of London were one of the decisive tipping points in the history of the 20th century. To this day the site remains extremely moving – hallowed ground infused with an intangible aura of national destiny.

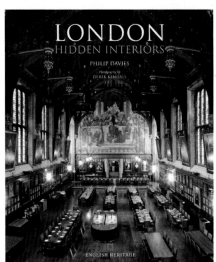

Philip Davies

As a chartered town planner, historian and international expert in heritage conservation, Philip Davies has been in the forefront of managing change to London's most important historic buildings and places for 40 years, most recently as the Planning and Development Director for London and South-East England at English Heritage. He has been instrumental in transforming some of Britain's most historic places including Trafalgar Square, Whitehall, Hyde Park Corner, Kings Cross/St Pancras, the British Museum, Woolwich Arsenal and Bletchley Park, as well as properties across the government estate and occupied royal palaces. He has prepared national policy and guidance on a whole range of topics from tall buildings to conservation-led regeneration.

Philip devised and set up English Heritage's buildings at risk programme in London as a result of which over 2,000 listed buildings have been saved from dereliction. He conceived and drove the Campaign for London's Squares, which has seen over twenty of London's most important squares restored to their original splendour, and pioneered English Heritage's Streets for All work to transform the public realm across the country.

Philip's most recent books, *Lost London, 1870-1945* and *Panoramas of Lost London* were published to huge acclaim, the former being shortlisted for the prestigious Spears Book Prize. Philip is a Fellow of the Society of Antiquaries, a Fellow of the Royal Historical Society, a Fellow of the Royal Asiatic Society, a Trustee of the Heritage of London Trust and a founder member of the International Advisory Group of the Yangon Heritage Trust, where he is advising on the conservation of one of the world's most important colonial cities.

London Hidden Interiors

1700 sumptuous photographs, many of them taken especially for this book, reveal in detail 180 of London's finest and most historic conserved interiors. Fascinating and informative accompanying text.
ISBN: 978-0-9568642-4-6; 448pp, £40

The majority of photographs in *London Hidden Interiors* were taken by Derek Kendall, until recently one of English Heritage's most senior staff photographers. Numerous images drawn from the existing archive needed to be refreshed because of renovations or refurbishment and Derek and other of his fellow EH staff photographers, James O Davies and Nigel Corrie provided the very latest images to make this book as up to date as possible. Richard Dumville, Charles Walker and Philip Davies all provided images from their personal collections.

Derek Kendall, Photographer

With over 40 years' experience Derek Kendall is one of the most talented and respected architectural and fine art photographers of his time. Benefiting from his intimate knowledge of London's built heritage and his exceptional eye for detail Derek's pictures have graced the pages of over 60 authoritative publications. His exhibitions include The City of London Churches at St Paul's Cathedral and The West End Theatres at the Victoria & Albert Museum.
